AF371905

BETYE SAAR

DRIFTING TOWARD TWILIGHT

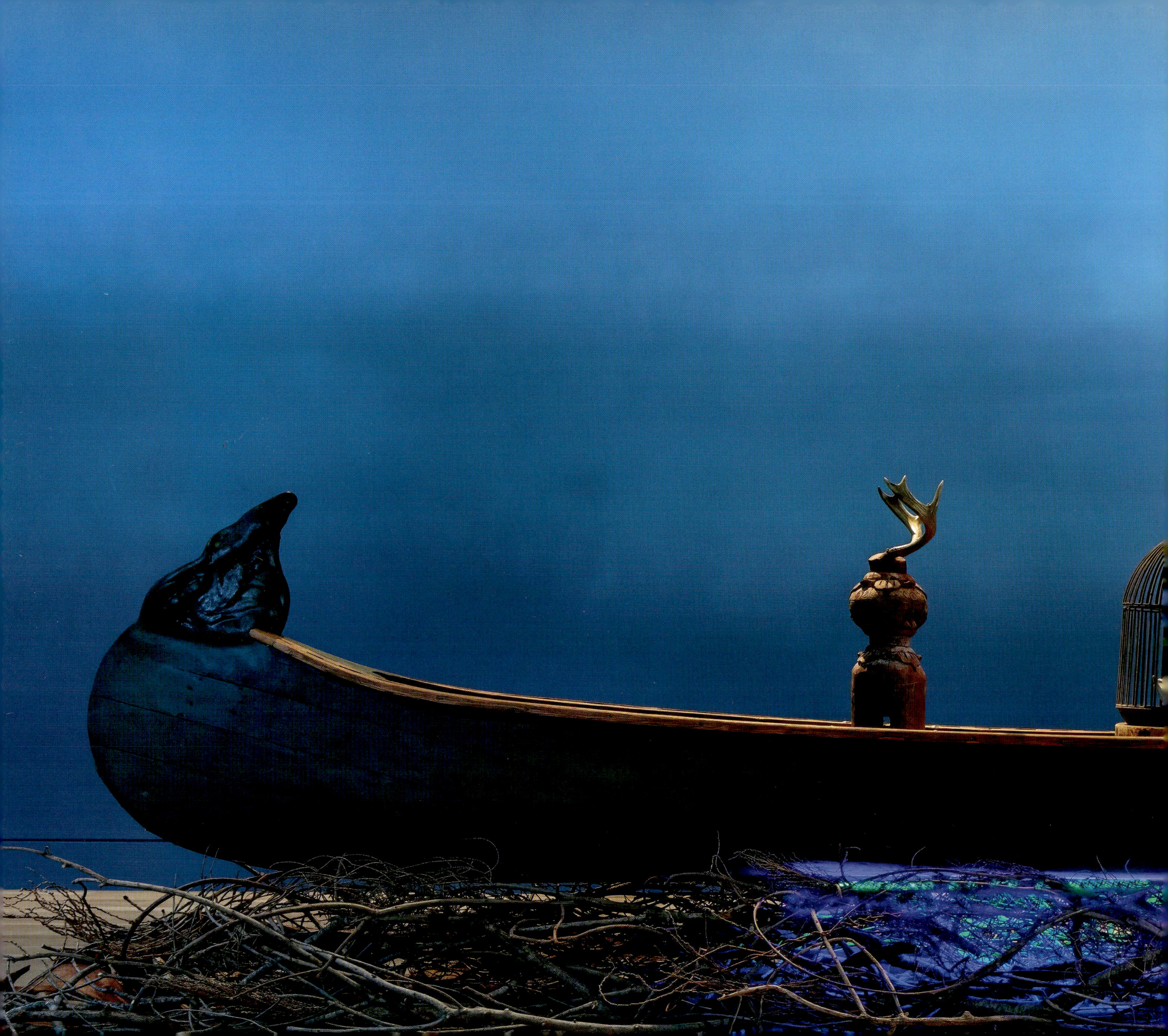

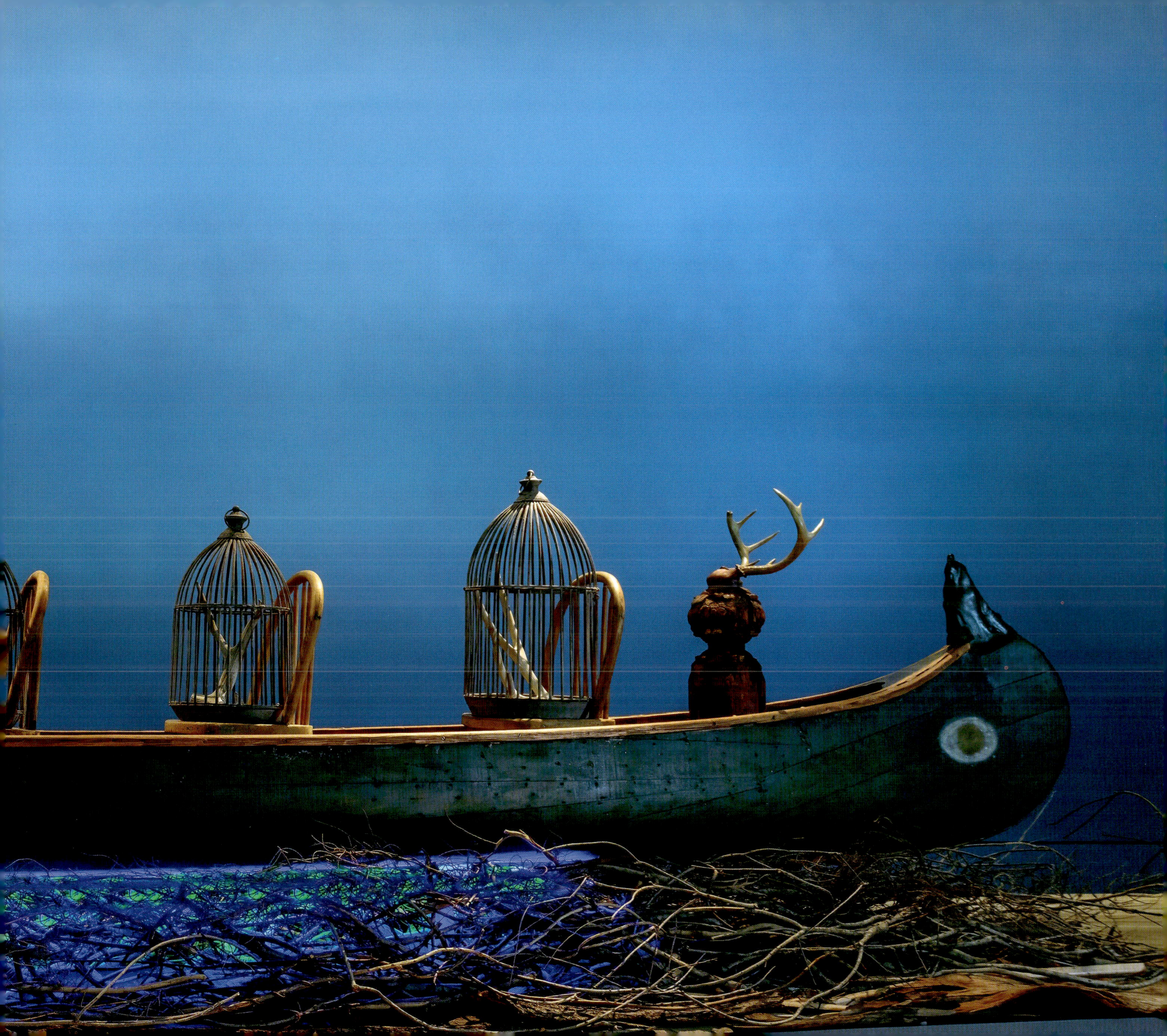

BETYE SAAR

edited by YINSHI LERMAN-TAN and SÓLA SAAR AGUSTSSON

with contributions by   HILTON ALS

TIFFANY E. BARBER

ISHMAEL REED

DRIFTING TOWARD TWILIGHT

THE HUNTINGTON LIBRARY, ART MUSEUM, AND BOTANICAL GARDENS

San Marino, California

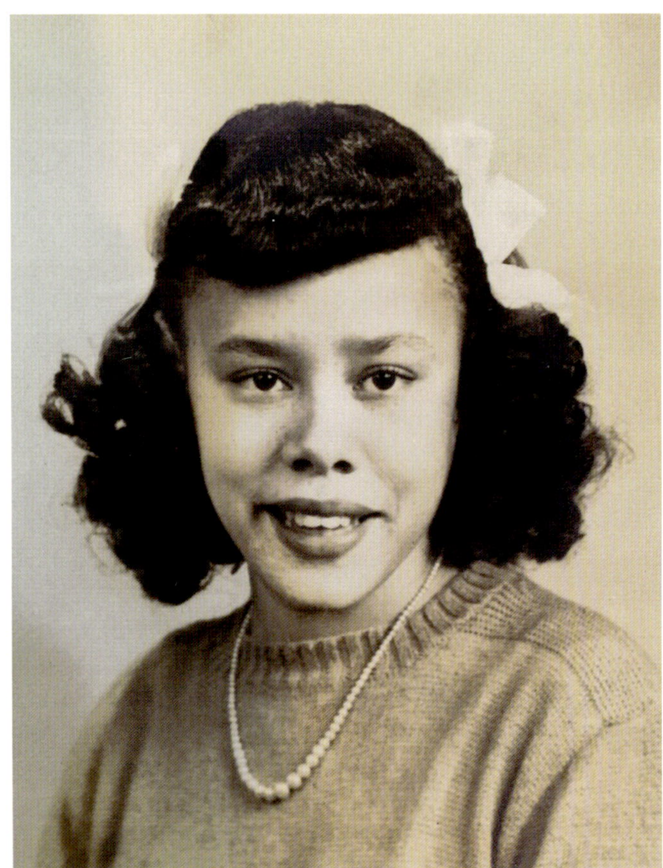

Betye Saar as a sophomore at
Pasadena Junior College, 1944.
Courtesy of the artist and Roberts
Projects, Los Angeles

I thought I was done with commissions and deadlines, which make making art less fun, but I couldn't resist saying yes to my new project for The Huntington museum, Drifting Toward Twilight. I'm from Pasadena and went to The Huntington as a child, so it's full-circle art.

—Betye Saar, 2024

CONTENTS

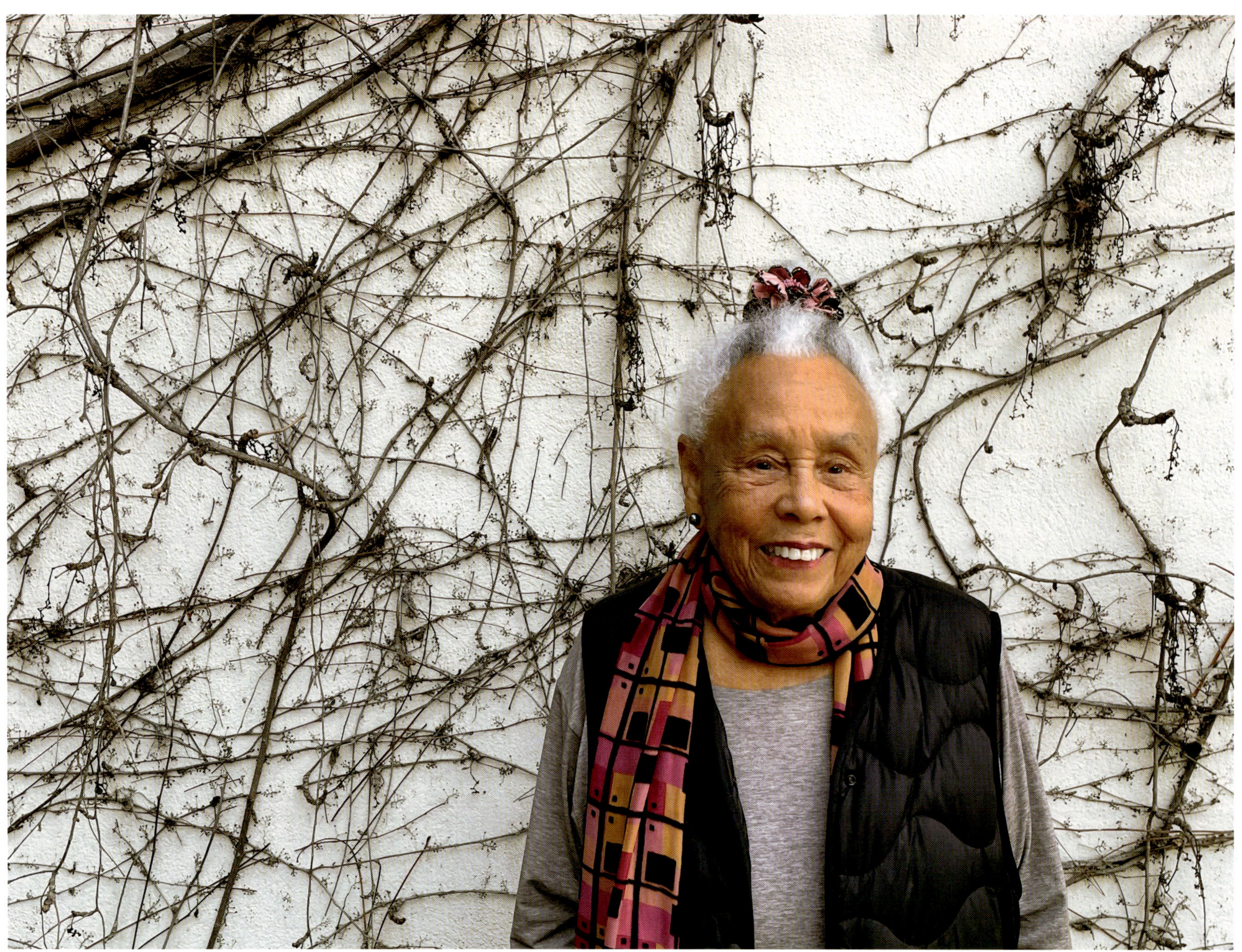

DIRECTOR'S FOREWORD

By bringing Betye Saar's immersive installation *Drifting Toward Twilight* into our galleries of American art, we are welcoming home a living legend who has deep roots in Pasadena and vivid memories of childhood visits to The Huntington. At age ninety-seven, her lust for life and delight in discovery were evident as she foraged our grounds for botanical materials to incorporate into the work. On strolls through our galleries, she paused repeatedly to sketch in a notebook, all the while dispensing pearls of wisdom to anyone within earshot, with disarming wit and a contagious smile.

During those moments with her, you could almost be forgiven for forgetting that you were in the presence of a genius. But make no mistake: she is a genius, by virtually any measure—a world-renowned icon, a breaker of barriers, and also a mother (of acclaimed artists) and grandmother (of promising writers and cultural creatives). And yet, through the newly completed artwork, in the last few days I have been reminded of the ancient meaning of the Latin word *genius*, which references an attendant spirit, a divine force or presence accompanying an individual through the journey that is life. I cannot help but marvel at the

Betye Saar at The Huntington, 2024

way Saar has conjured up the spirits dormant in quotidian objects—a canoe, children's chairs, fallen tree branches—and breathed into them a new life. She has long referenced different spiritual and religious practices in her work, but is she herself an attendant spirit to each of us, encouraging us to see the world differently?

We are deeply grateful to Betye Saar herself, for agreeing to the project and for delighting us at every turn throughout the ideation and implementation process. Betye Saar's studio manager, Tracye Saar-Cavanaugh, and gallerist Julie Roberts of Roberts Projects offered unfailing support and great advice. Julie Roberts and her team generously shared deep knowledge of and access to the archival materials from the Betye Saar papers, as well as rare early artworks, to richly illustrate this catalogue. Betye and Tracye graciously provided precious family photos and histories. Alison Saar and Lezley Saar also supported the team; Robert Hori, Lise East, and the Botanical Gardens staff helped with foraging; and Kyle Provencio Reingold, Neil Howard Butler, and Gloria S. Álvarez produced a marvelous film that captures the arc of Saar's career, her fierce determination and kind intelligence, and her connections to Pasadena and The Huntington.

We are also deeply grateful to a number of Huntington colleagues who have helped make her vision a reality. The Huntington's president, Karen Lawrence, and the trustees supported this initiative from the beginning. Many others contributed time and expertise: Chief Curator of American Art Dennis Carr and Gail-Oxford Associate Curator of American Art Lauren Cross; Elizabeth Clingerman in the Director's Office; Cynthia Tovar, Lindsey Hansen, and Pat Pickett in Registration and Collections Management; Mark Jones, Anders Lansing, Sheila Salley, Sean Kennedy, Thomas Cabbell, and Joe Leavenworth in Preparations; Lana Johnson, Angela Fann, Danielle Killam, and Jesson Duller in Exhibitions; Jean Patterson and Shirin Sadjadpour in Publications; Randy Shulman, Sarah Basile, Pam Hearn, and Emily Goldblatt in Advancement; Janet Alberti, Patty Hanna, and Patrick Plasterer in Finance; Holly Moore, Kristi Westberg, Megan Caloca, and Christina O'Connell in Preservation and Conservation; and Thea Page and Jessica McCormack in Communications. And outside The Huntington, many thanks go to Mary Skarbek at Roberts Projects; Marci Boudreau and Robert Creighton at Picnic Design; and Michael Flechtner, Buro Happold, and Lutron Electronics.

The co-curators for the project, Yinshi Lerman-Tan and Sóla Saar Agustsson, worked their own kind of magic, navigating the artist's creative process and institutional procedures with remarkable results. Lerman-Tan brought art historical bona fides and fangirl admiration, while Agustsson mined her lifetime of experience with Saar as both an artworld icon and a grandmother, or "GrandBetye," as she calls her.

For generous support of this project, which made it all possible, special thanks go to Mei-Lee Ney, the Philip and Muriel Berman Foundation, Terry Perucca and Annette Serrurier, Faye and Robert C. Davidson Jr., and the Virginia Steele Scott Foundation.

Christina Nielsen
Hannah and Russel Kully Director of the Art Museum

Betye Saar, *Drifting Toward Twilight*, 2023 (installation view with the artist). Mixed media installation. The Huntington Library, Art Museum, and Botanical Gardens. Commissioned through Roberts Projects, Los Angeles. This acquisition was made possible by a leadership gift from Mei-Lee Ney. Major support was also provided by the Philip and Muriel Berman Foundation, Terry Perucca and Annette Serrurier, Faye and Robert C. Davidson Jr., and the Virginia Steele Scott Endowment for American Art, 2023.15

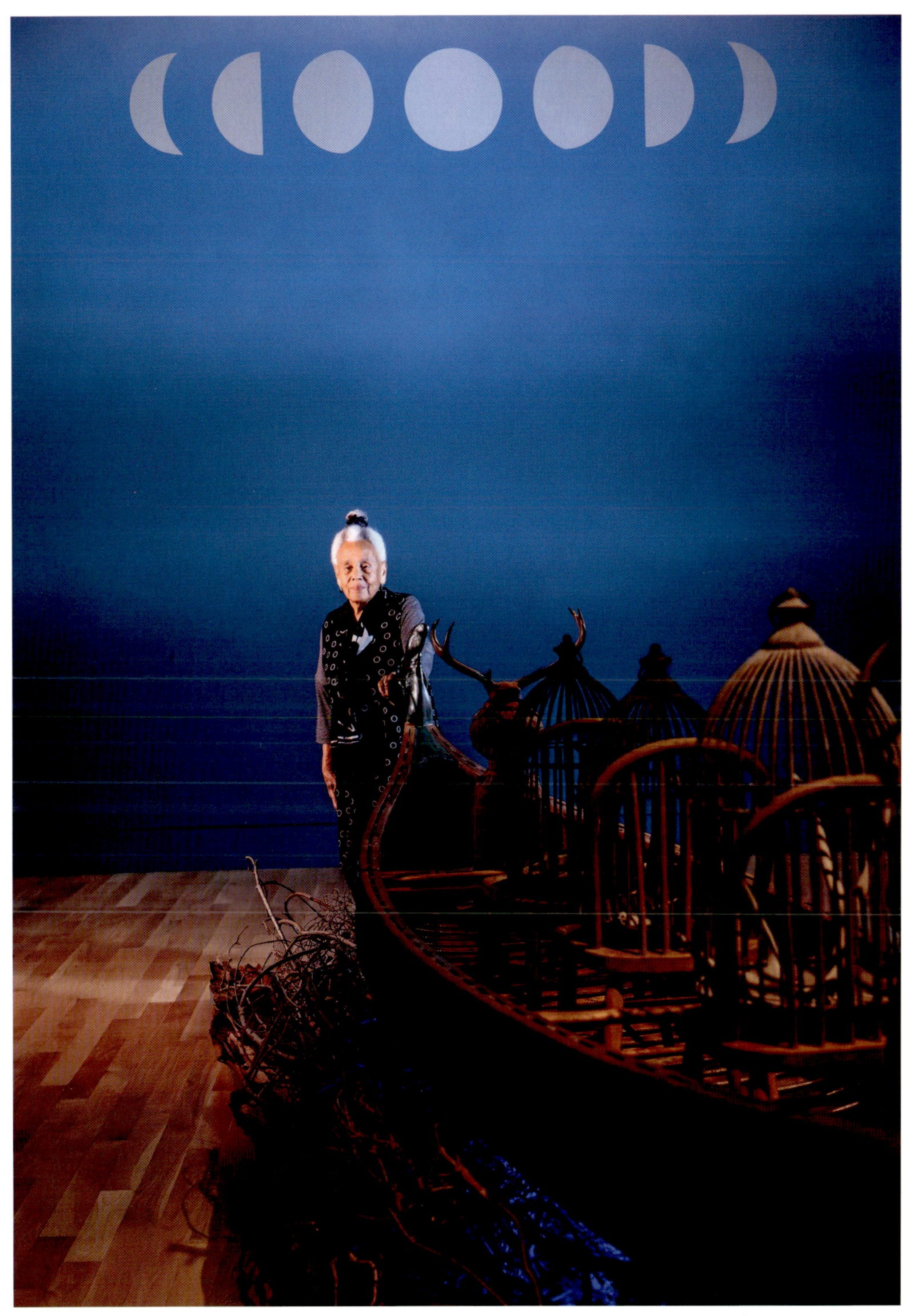

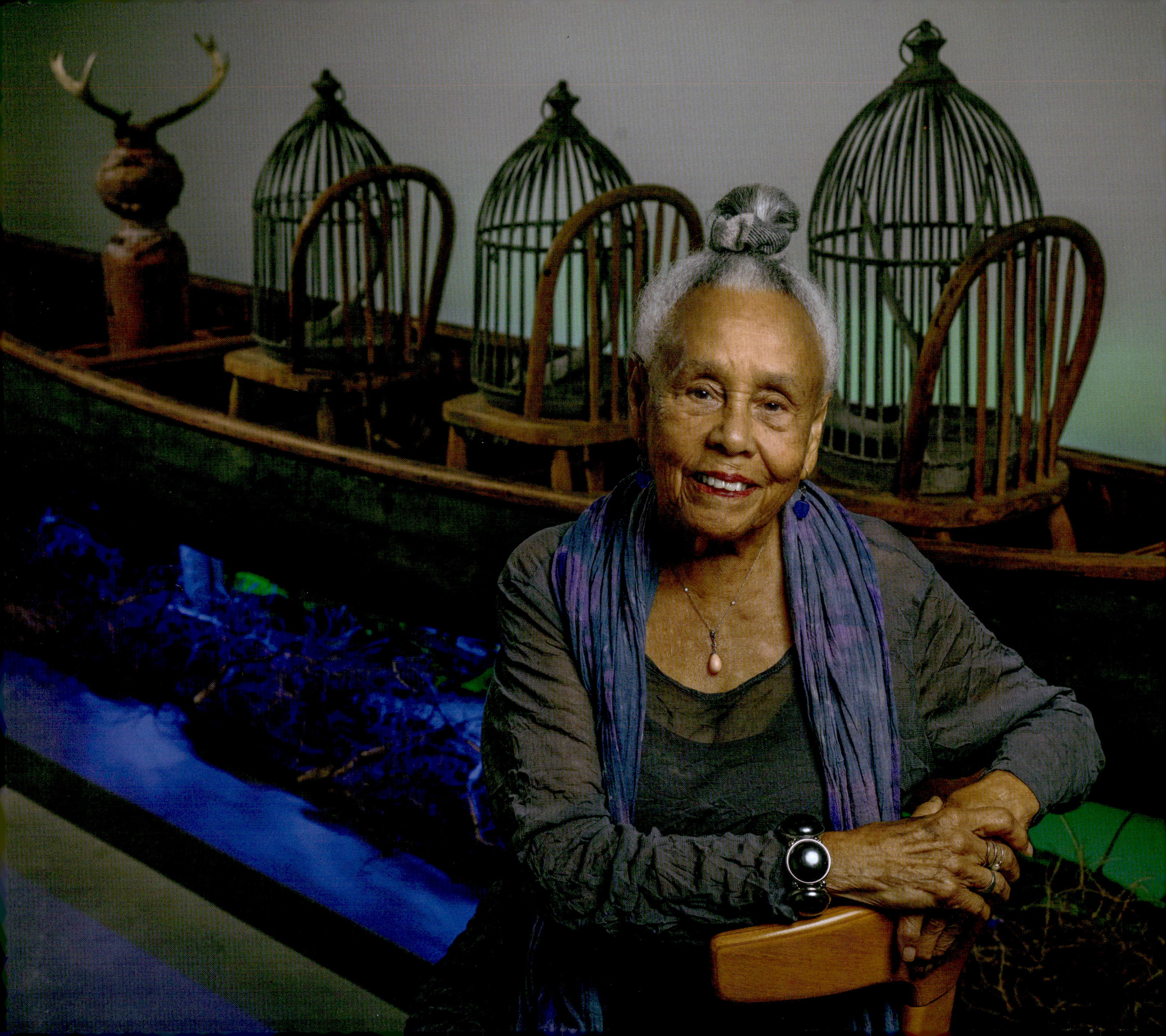

ISHMAEL REED

TEETERING TOWARD GREATNESS

On March 10, 2023, I picked up 2,400 photos that were sent to my archives. They include pictures of artists, actors, and politicians I've encountered—for example, Congressman Charlie Rangel and me partying at Minton's in Harlem. During their trip to Oakland, I also posed with choreographer and dancer Bill T. Jones at a New York gallery and with Dizzy Gillespie and Max Roach. There are photos I took of Alvin Ailey, Mike Tyson, Muhammad Ali, Dick Gregory, and others.

There are some photos that I missed. One was the meeting of Betye Saar with Adrienne Kennedy. They could be twins. They share an aesthetic, which I call Afro-Gothicism. They share a style with Henry Dumas, Toni Morrison, Sun Ra, and Thelonious Monk. All view Black history as a ghost story. Their works reflect a high level of spookiness. The past and the present intersect. Ancestors are contemporary. Ordinary materials, like advertisements and popular movies, might exist alongside Shakespeare or Buddha. They are supreme parodists and ironists.

Though both are in their nineties, they continue to produce. Adrienne Kennedy made Broadway in 2022, and Betye Saar continues to receive recognition, most

recently from Harvard University. In 2019, Saar was honored at LACMA [Los Angeles County Museum of Art], and a photo showed Leonardo DiCaprio at her table, paying tribute. Both Betye and Adrienne were able to overcome tokenism as a result of beautiful genes and extraordinary talent. They've seen others come and go. They have consistently produced enough high-quality work to teeter toward greatness.

Betye and I have collaborated since the 1970s. She drew controversy when she replaced a white Amazon queen who appears on the California state seal with a Black queen (p. 17). Though the Black figure was based on both Gallic and Spanish legends portraying Calafia as Black, after the book was published, I received a complaint from a librarian who said she was a seventh-generation Californian and wanted to keep California spic and span. "Lady," I said, "you're three thousand years too late." Since then, I've learned that the three thousand number was conservative. The librarian's comment reflects the kind of Ethnic Chauvinism that artists like Saar and Kennedy have faced. It took Kennedy longer to reach Broadway because Broadway could only anoint one Black playwright at a time. The

Betye Saar with *Drifting Toward Twilight*, 2023. Courtesy of the artist and Roberts Projects, Los Angeles

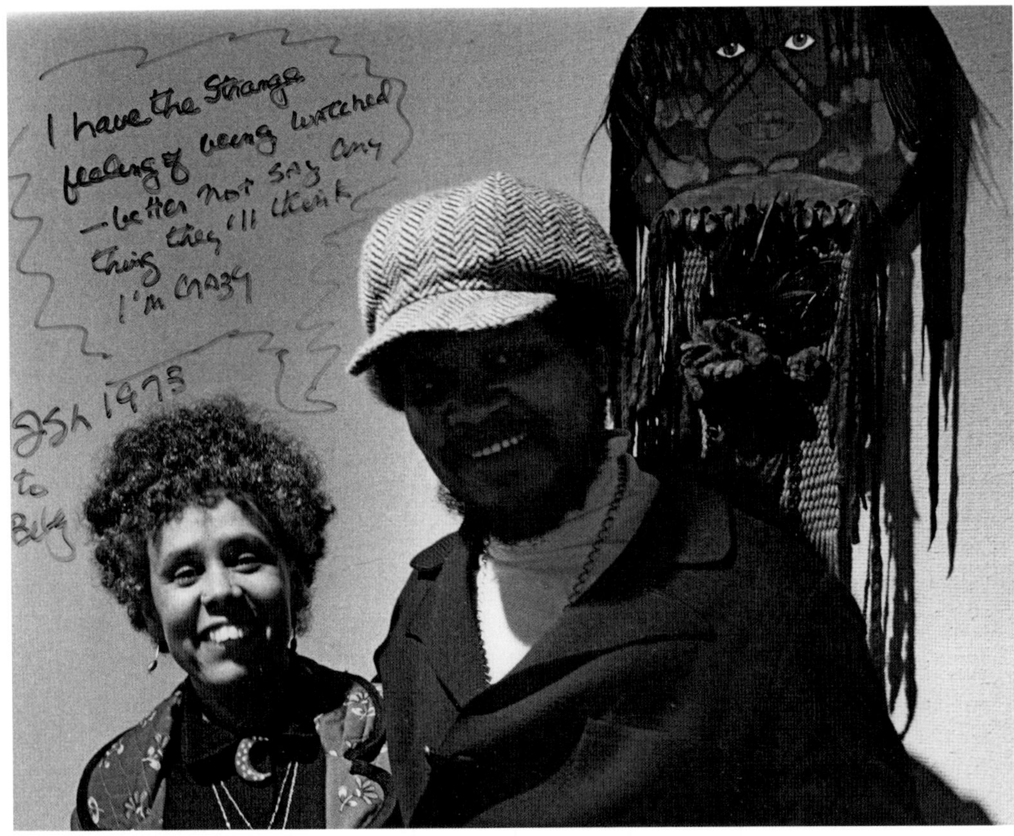

Betye Saar and Ishmael Reed at the Berkeley Art Center, Berkeley, California, with Saar's artwork *Gelede* behind them, 1973. Inscribed by Reed. Courtesy of the artist and Roberts Projects, Los Angeles

museums pit Saar against a younger artist who, though very talented, is one-dimensional.

One-dimensional Betye Saar is not. She rejected demands made by galleries that Black artists disappear into the opaque abyss of Abstract Expressionism. Since her early work, she has taken the route of the unbossed maverick. She transformed the racist images vomited up from some sick and tormented souls that can be found in ads and photos into works of art. She recasts the "Mammy" nurturer, an object of endearment in the South and the North long honored in Hollywood and on Broadway, fetishized and worshipped. Nelson Algren even reports that white johns who required Black prostitutes to assume the role of the Mammy were called "black-Mammy freaks." Professor Eric Sundquist sent me a copy of a resolution passed by white Southern senators that saluted the Mammy. It's an entry in the Congressional Record. In one of Saar's most famous works, *The Liberation of Aunt Jemima* (1972), Aunt Jemima is no passive, shuffling creature or object of erotic fantasies held by plantation adolescents, but armed (see p. 38).

Her *Black Girl's Window* (1969) tells the situation of Black women in America looking out at Nordic standards for beauty (see p. 26). This was before Black models were featured in the leading fashion magazines. However, some bottom-feeding politicians can still win elections by darkening images of their Black opponent's skin in campaign ads.

It took a lot of courage for Betye Saar to transform these images from the source of such shame among the conservative Black middle class. The Harlem

BETYE SAAR

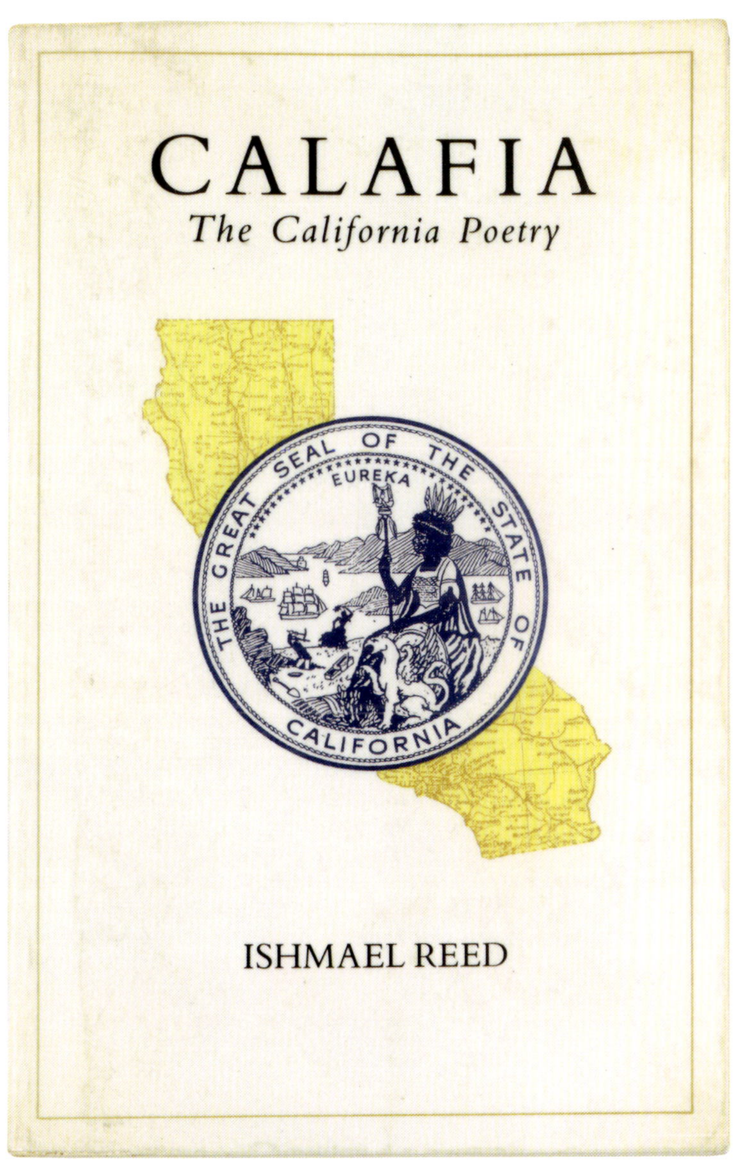

Betye Saar, cover artwork for *Calafia: The California Poetry* (1979) by Ishmael Reed. Courtesy of the artist and Roberts Projects, Los Angeles

Renaissance thought it had gotten rid of Aunts and Uncles. Why is Betye Saar bringing them back? Larry Neal and Amiri Baraka challenged the white aesthetic. But the ads that Betye Saar transforms and comments upon are more representative of the white aesthetic than Faulkner, who, for Larry Neal, epitomized the white aesthetic. In a pathetic attempt at esteem, Blacks and others had to be demeaned. Yet, whites helped themselves to Black creations like ragtime.

Both Kennedy and Saar overcame the kind of Ethnic Chauvinism that led one writer to call a talented contemporary white writer "The Voice of the West," when Hispanic writers have produced literature in the West since the 1600s, and Native Americans have been telling stories for thousands of years.

I have learned from Native Americans. Poet Joy Harjo reminds us that some Native American cultures have been crushed by Anglo domination. Carla Blank and I published the last story of one Northwest Coast tribe whose language disappeared when the previous speaker died. Currently, there is an effort by white chauvinists to do what their counterparts in museums, through exclusivity, have failed to do: outlaw Black culture. Betye Saar, like Hale Woodruff, Aaron Douglas, Jacob Lawrence, and Romare Bearden, has kept Black culture extant. They are not only great artists but also archivists and teachers.

✶ ● ✶

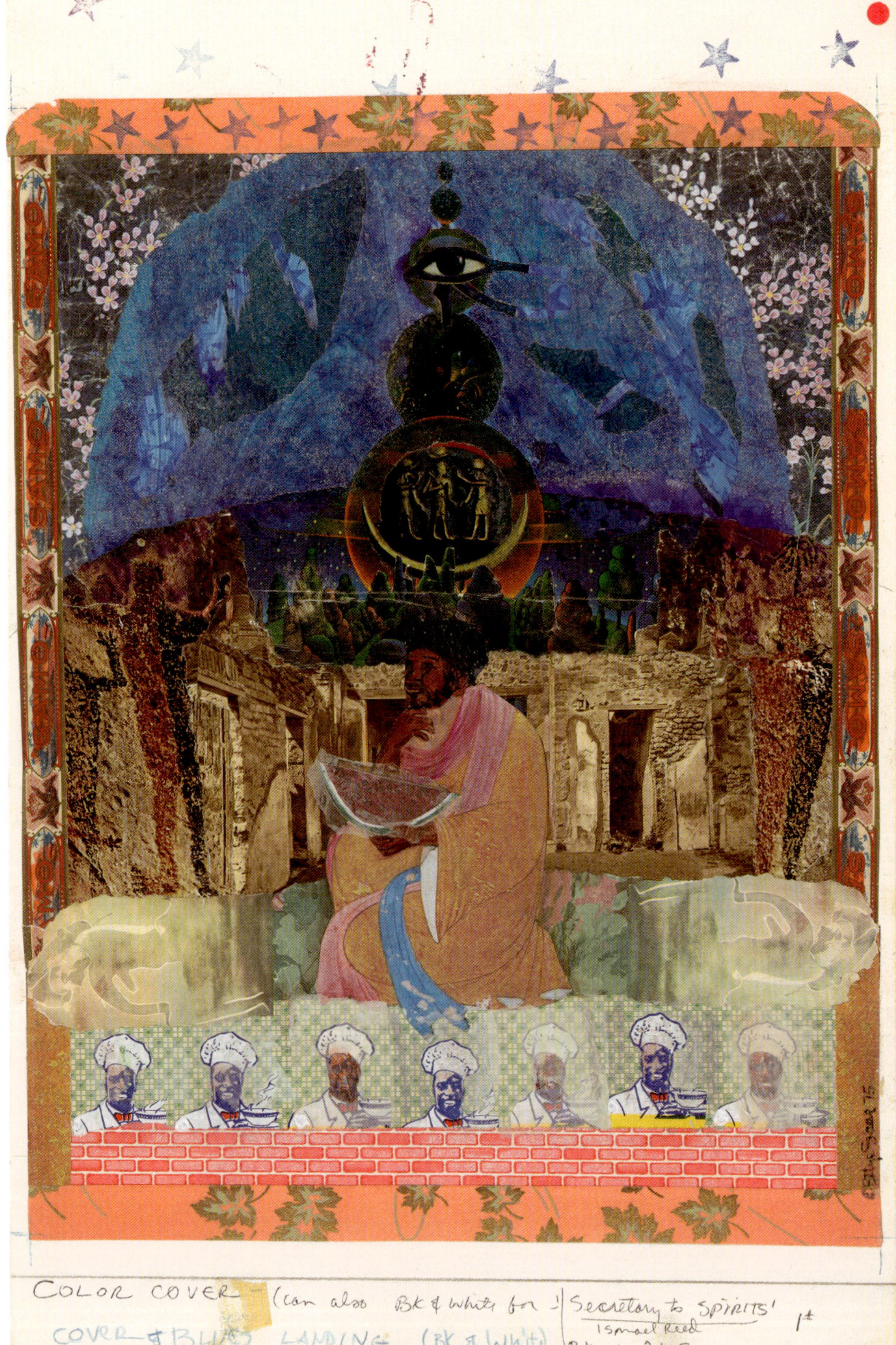

Betye Saar, *A Secretary to the Spirits*, 1975. Collage of cut printed papers and fabrics, with matte and metallic paint and ink stamps on laminated paperboard, 15 × 10 in. (38.1 × 25.4 cm). Commission for *A Secretary to the Spirits* (1978) by Ishmael Reed. The Morgan Library & Museum, New York, Gift of the Modern and Contemporary Collectors Committee, 2017, 2017.306:1

BETYE SAAR

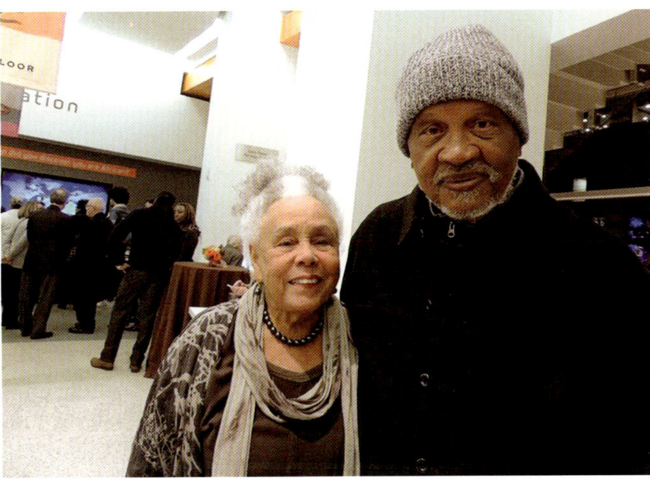

Betye Saar and Ishmael Reed at the Museum of the African Diaspora, San Francisco, 2015

At eighty-five, I find that people I used to party with have streets, landmarks, and institutions named for them. I knew them at their most relaxed. We had some good times together.

Betye illustrated my book *A Secretary to the Spirits* (facing page). We were the only Americans on the list of publications from Joseph Okpaku's NOK, a Nigerian publishing house. Little did we know at the time that fifty years later, the book would become a classic. We were featured in an exhibit held by the Morgan Library and in a recent *New York Times* issue.

For both Betye and Adrienne, it has been a long journey but one in which they triumphed. That's because, as a boxing trainer told me when I asked why Muhammad Ali had won a fight: "Class will tell."

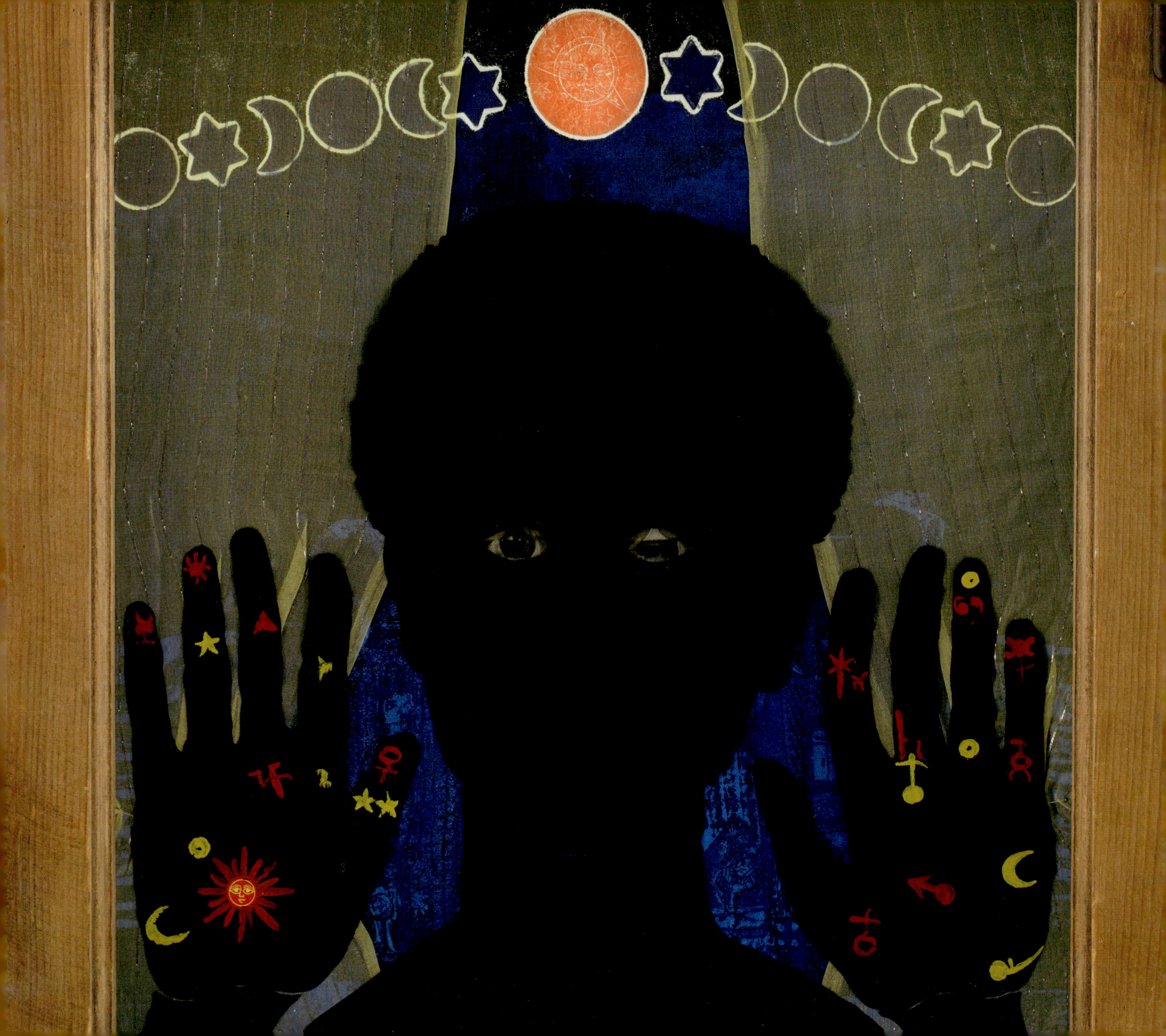

BETYE SAAR, ARTIST

The following is an interview Ishmael Reed conducted with Betye Saar in 1973 on the occasion of her exhibition Black Girl's Window *at the Berkeley Art Center, Berkeley, California, originally published in his 1978 book of essays,* Shrovetide in Old New Orleans.

Betye Saar is a working mother who skitters about California in a Saab usually accompanied by the three daughters she raised: Alison, seventeen, Tracye, twelve, and Lezley, twenty, a student at San Francisco City College. She is the recipient of awards from the Downey Museum of Art, Downey, California; the Fifth Annual California Small Image Exhibition; the Pasadena Artists' Society; the Watts Summer Festival; the Los Angeles County Museum of Art; and the Whitney Museum of American Art, New York City, and her work is included in major American collections—private and museum. She has designed costumes for theater and motion pictures, and has made two films: *Colored Spade* and *Eyeball* (p. 25). Her work draws its sources from Africa, Oceania, as well as Afro-American folklore. The following interview was conducted in March 1973, after the completion of her successful show at Berkeley's Live Oak Park.

Detail of Betye Saar, *Black Girl's Window* (p. 26)

ISHMAEL REED: Betye, why do you call your show, your recent successful show, *Black Girl's Window*?

BETYE SAAR: Well, actually the gallery director thought of that title, after that window that I have—it's kind of a takeoff from a line by Matisse, which is "Art is a window . . . a way of sharing. . . ." And that was kind of like my whole feeling about the show—the way I see things. Like looking out from my head, from my eyes, and the way the viewer sees. And since the majority of the works were windows, that's why we decided on that theme.

IR: Is this the reason you have a play on many kinds of eyes? I notice a persistent element in your work was the eye—the Egyptian eye—different kinds of eyes. Done on leather and using all kinds of materials to construct an eye (p. 24). You've talked about the seeing, the idea of the visual and seeing through a window.

BS: It relates in part to that. I have selected certain symbols that I repeat in my work, and the eye is one. And the eye also serves as looking at one, or one sees

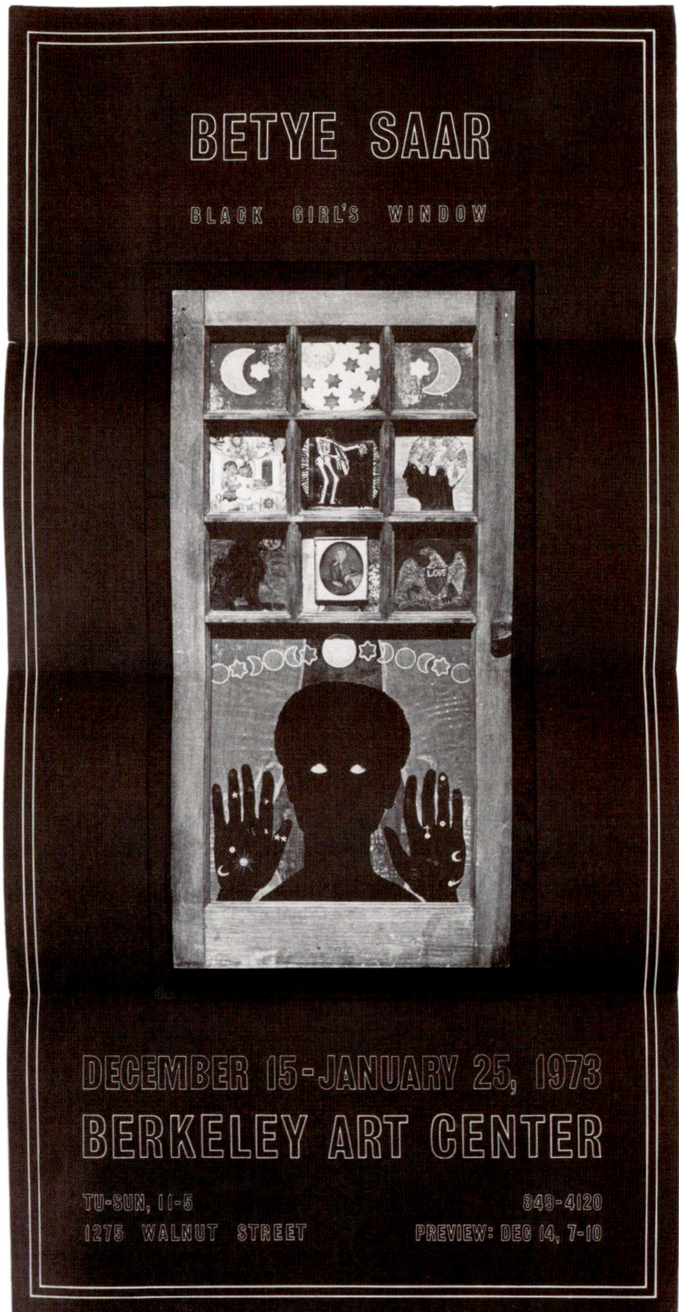

Black Girl's Window exhibition poster, Berkeley Art Center, Berkeley, California, 1972–73. Courtesy of the artist and Roberts Projects, Los Angeles

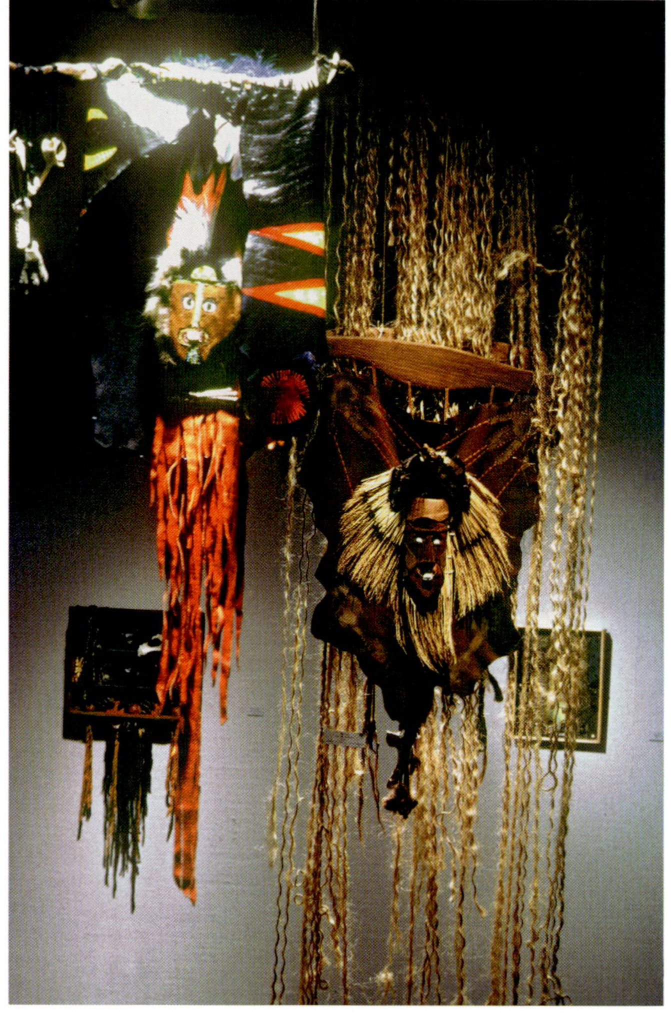

Black Girl's Window (installation view), Berkeley Art Center, Berkeley, California, 1972–73. Courtesy of the artist and Roberts Projects, Los Angeles

BETYE SAAR

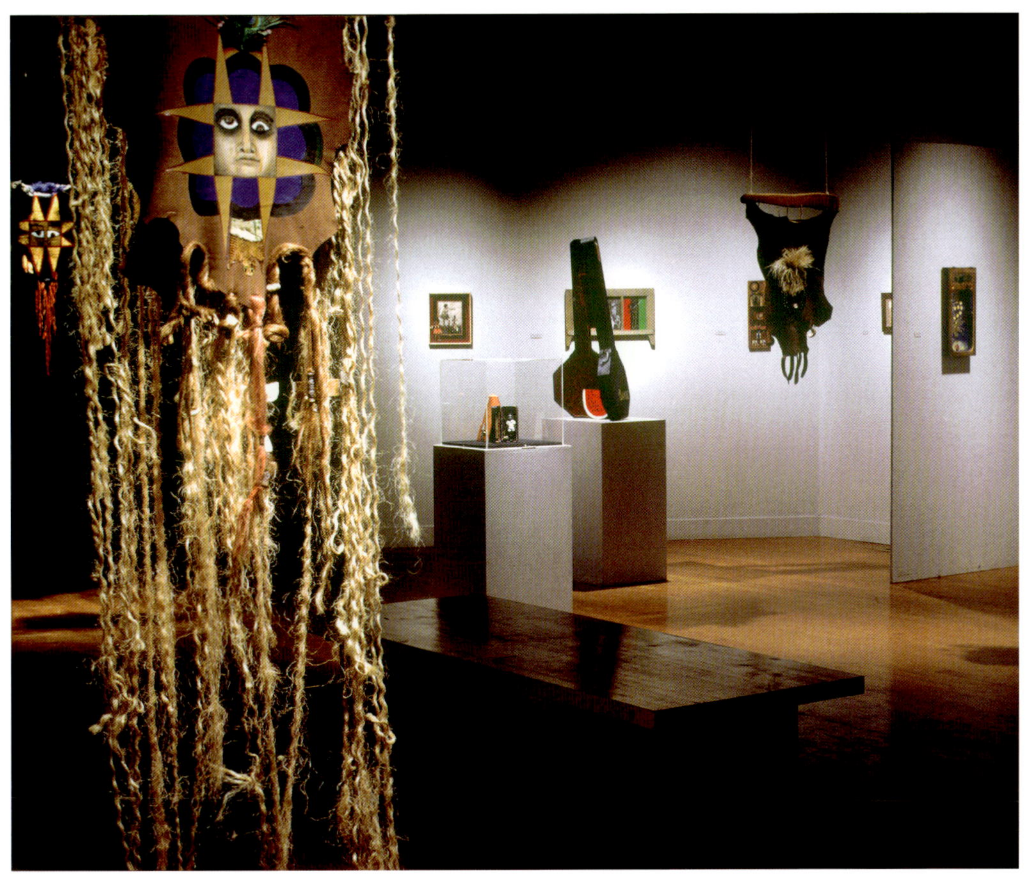

Black Girl's Window (installation view), Berkeley Art Center, Berkeley, California, 1972–73. Courtesy of the artist and Roberts Projects, Los Angeles

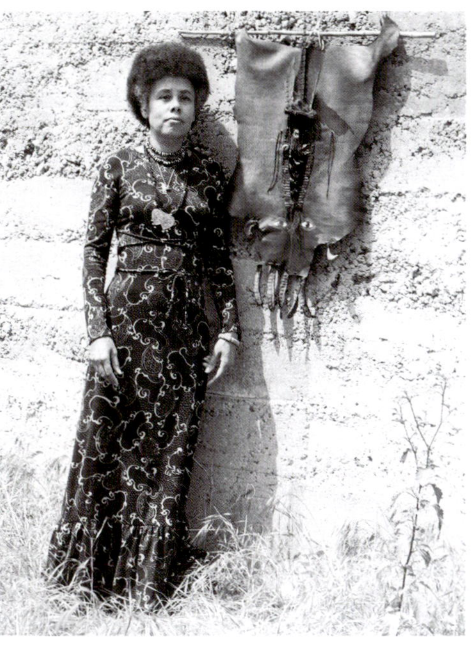

Betye Saar in her Laurel Canyon backyard with *John the Conqueror*, 1971. Courtesy of the artist and Roberts Projects, Los Angeles

the same thing as one eye sees another eye. It's true I use the Egyptian eye, which is the "all-seeing eye," the protective eye to ward off the "evil eye." I like the form, the shape, the design of the eye. And I use many materials—paint, rocks, eye shapes—openings—this means a looking out, an attitude as well as the graphic image.

IR: In my mind I mentally divided your work into three or four series—this particular show we're discussing. One section of it dealt with the way blacks have been depicted, especially in entertainment and in popular culture. And to achieve this effect you used elements like, for example, a real banjo, and you used old advertisements for toothpaste, and things like that—soap—

things that give an ironic commentary on history. Then at the same time you're able to take essential forms that one sees in a survey—you know—of a history of blacks in America and connect them with what's going on now. For example, I saw one piece you had in which two people were holding banjos and the final—it was like a triptych—and the final panel showed a man with a rifle. Were you saying that things haven't changed very much in history?

BS: The title of that piece is *Let Me Entertain You*. And my reason for that window was that the black in his traditional role has been the entertainer—the dancing darky, the banjo player, or whatever—that was the first panel of that window. The second panel was a

　　　DRIFTING TOWARD TWILIGHT

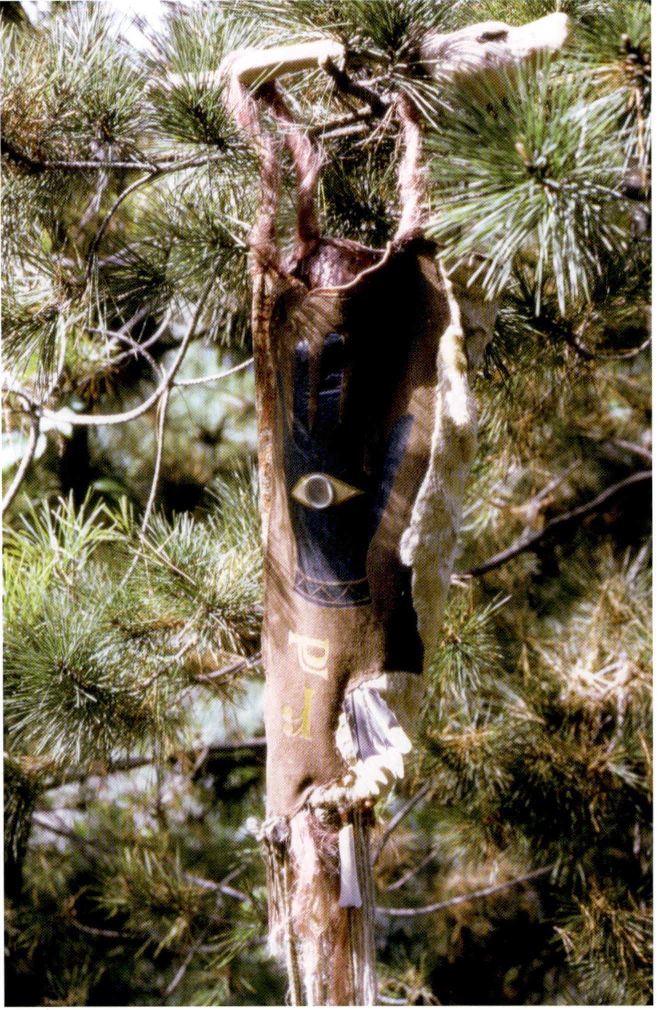

Betye Saar, *Mojo Bag #1 Hand*, 1970. Mixed media assemblage, 62 × 17 × 2 in. (157.5 × 43.2 × 5.1 cm). Los Angeles County Museum of Art, Purchased with funds provided by Alice and Nahum Lainer, the Modern Art Acquisition Fund, the Modern and Contemporary Art Council, the Laurie M. Tisch Illumination Fund in honor of Betye Saar and Steve Tisch, Francis H. Williams and Keris A. Salmon, H. Allen Evans and Anna Rosicka, and Kim and Keith Allen-Niesen, M.2019.286. Courtesy of the artist and Roberts Projects, Los Angeles

This artwork was included in the 1972–73 exhibition Black Girl's Window, *Berkeley Art Center, Berkeley, California, where Saar and Reed first met.*

lynch scene, which is another form of white entertainment. So the reverse is that there's a new form of entertainment—the black's entertainment. (I guess it could be interpreted as that.) And instead of the musical instrument, the instrument is now a rifle. The reason for the black imagery is—well, it started three or four years ago, and I started collecting those images in postcards and sheet music, and other forms of advertisements—I guess it was around the turn of the century when a lot of that was prevalent. So many of those images were hurtful. I mean really painful, like a watermelon that explodes and there's like a nigger's head in it—that kind of thing. Just horrible jokes and things. This is a really negative thing, and how can I, as an artist, change that to make it into a positive thing, to make it a thing of beauty, a thing of interest? So I started using those images in my work.

And then a kind of revolution or social statement evolved from that—it's because I worked in a kind of stream of consciousness way, things just fall into place. And it just seems to come out that way—that it [turns into] revolution, and it also has—but this idea didn't come to me until after I had finished several works, and I could look back at them and say, "Hey, I'm kind of in a trance and this is my creative revolution because I can't participate any other way," I just can't because of my makeup and my personality. So I do it this way. And this also serves as an explanation to whites or others as to why blacks react the way they are because they have all that [hate] behind them.

IR: You know, you said something very interesting. You said you worked on a stream of consciousness level, but there is an order in your work—a consistency and a kind of rationalism, but maybe a different kind of rationalism—a kind of reasoning that may not be able to explain—as beyond reason. You understand what I mean?

BS: Sure.

IR: I mean there may be another order, and you may be one of these unique individuals who are gifted to tap

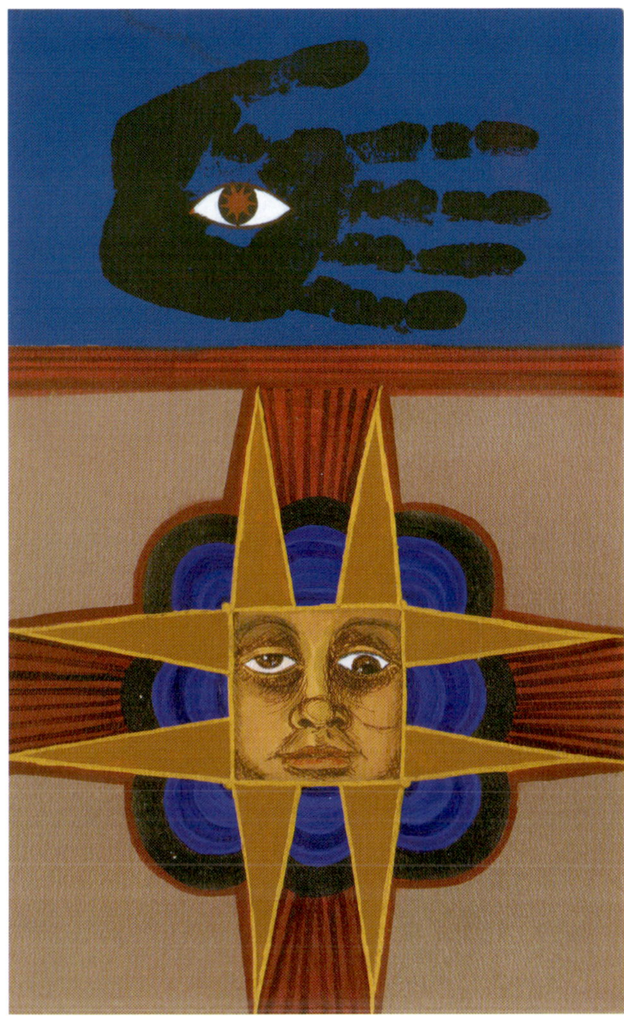

Betye Saar, *The Divine Face and Hand*, 1971. Acrylic, gouache, and ink on paper, 14⅜ × 9 in. (36.5 × 22.9 cm). The Museum of Modern Art, New York, Promised gift of Candace King Weir, PG87.2021. Courtesy of the artist and Roberts Projects, Los Angeles

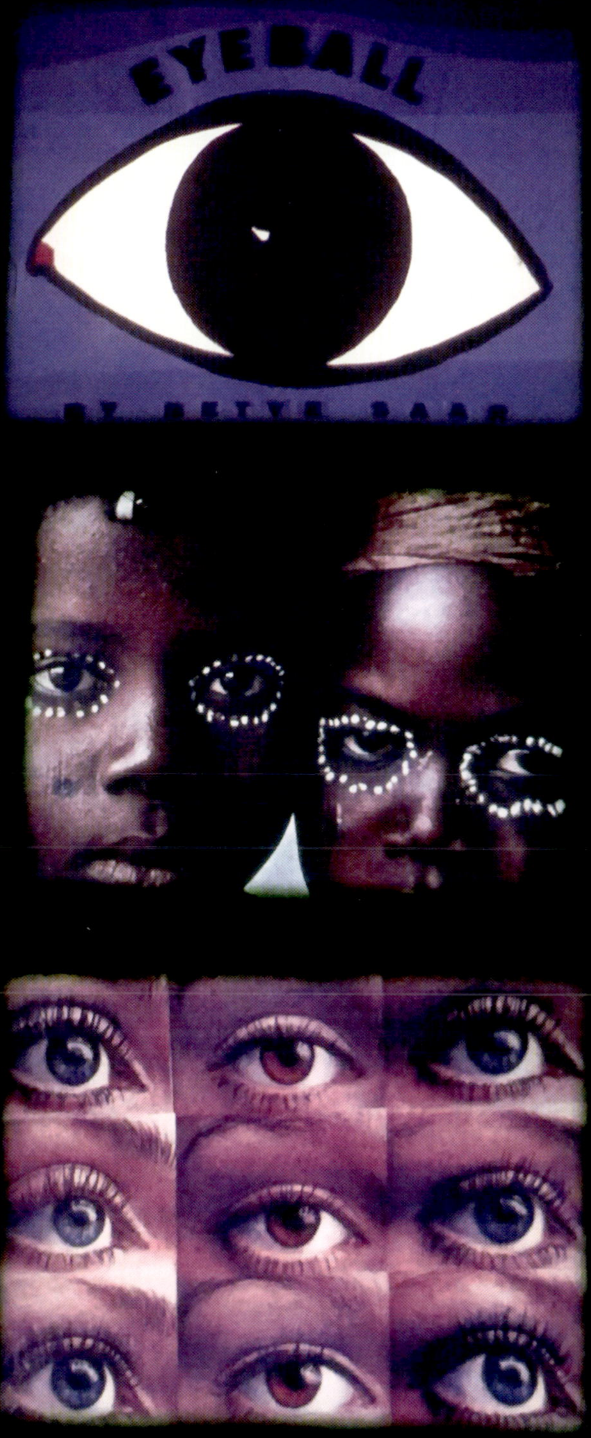

Betye Saar, film stills from *Eyeball*, 1971. Courtesy of the artist and Roberts Projects, Los Angeles

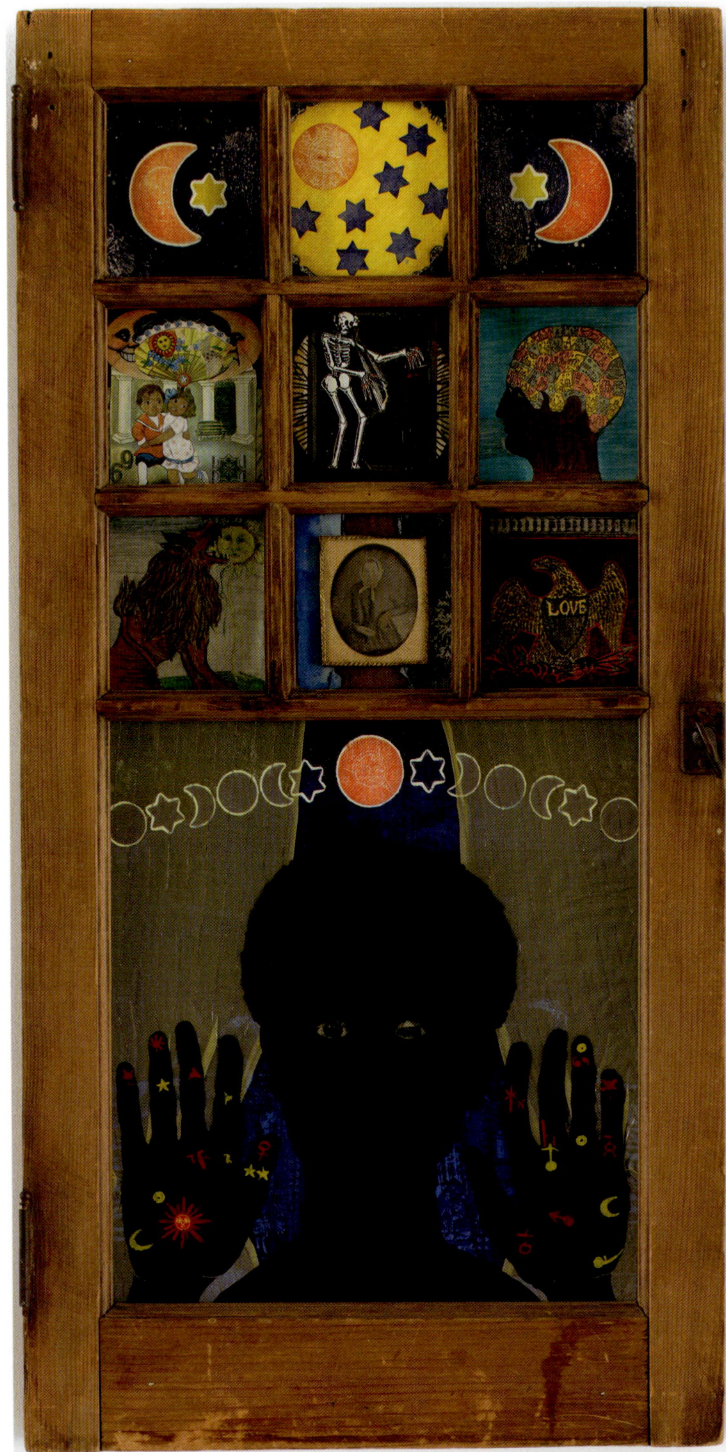

Betye Saar, *Black Girl's Window*, 1969. Wooden window frame with paint, cut-and-pasted printed and painted papers, daguerreotype, lenticular print, and plastic figurine, 35¾ × 18 × 1½ in. (90.8 × 45.7 × 3.8 cm). The Museum of Modern Art, New York, Gift of Candace King Weir through The Modern Women's Fund, and Committee on Painting and Sculpture Funds, 549.2013

another dimension, another universe, or a world most of us aren't able to see yet! You do use a lot of ideas, and in your work you use objects that we associate with—for want of a better term—African religion. Do you see yourself in that tradition?

BS: Well, my art is very personal. It's like what is in my head at the time I'm doing it, although several pieces are worked on at the same time. About this stream of consciousness thing, I do tap a source because in the last two years I have developed a technique from a technique that was taught to me of using the alpha and the theta brain waves for creativity. And it's like a kind of self-hypnosis where you get rid of all the input of other shit that's going around and just let it flow. And it's so automatic that you're not even conscious that it's happening. I don't have any trial-and-error kind of business. Sometimes two things really catch my eye, but in the end I always really know the right one. About the African thing, it's not so much African as what we call Primitive, because I use Egyptian and Oceanic and American Indian and African, any kind of culture that is related more to the earth or to nature and I use those kinds of materials. That's where that theory comes from, that evolves with putting materials and symbols and colors together so that in one piece you may find materials or symbols or signs or designs from several cultures, but it all works together as a tribal thing. But then, it's a secret tribe.

IR: So then it's like Betye Saar's window and not a black girl's window.

BETYE SAAR

BS: Right.

IR: I want to get back to this series that really interested me. I thought the other work was craftsman's work—one of the series was leather—and designs painted on leather. That was so intricate to me that I thought that it would take someone who went through the process of doing that to really appreciate it, because I could see there were different kinds of knitting involved. You must have gotten into like the encyclopedia of world knitting to put that together like that. It is an Afro-American tradition because you took bird feathers and you took organic material and you took found material and you linked it up together. It's a very sophisticated version of the old quilt making in the Afro-American South, where the women would use disparate materials and make a quilt, which was like one unity. But that series, I guess I like it because it was very literary. For example, you had a panel, you had four panels—cartoon panels on the washboard.

BS: *National Washboard.*

IR: Yeah, and so you do use this in some instances to create a debunking effect on American history as we see it. I notice, for example, you use authentic photographs from the same period that the caricatures were derived from. So you saw how things were actually at that time and how they'd been caricatured. So do I see like some muckraking going on?

BS: Right, right. The series that I have—they're like the tribal things, like the past. So far I've been dealing mostly in the past and in the future and some of the things in the past touch the present, like in the *Black* series. Like they have the panel with the revolution and things like that. In [the] one you're speaking of, *National Washboard*—the washboard itself was a symbol of the black woman—her Aunt Jemima role and the washerwoman, whatever. And it was a cartoon series from a newspaper [to] which I added collage—I took words out and added the watermelon and the Aunt Jemima head and things like that. And on the other side of that—because that piece is exhibited suspended—there's a black hand and a red fist, a clenched fist, which give the other side of the washboard scene, or the other side of the coin.

IR: There was another one you're speaking of, the Aunt Jemima figure, the archetype which you find in other work of yours. I saw a few of those images. In one you had the two measuring cups and in the one measuring cup there appeared to be flour and in the other measuring cup it appeared to be dynamite.

BS: Right. That's *Measure for Measure.* And also behind that *Aunt Jemima's Finest Flour* and on the other side was *Revolution* or *Africa* or *Right On*—or whatever.

IR: It was a very versatile show. Many people get into a rut, but I could see where you experiment with different ideas and different cultures and different media. You had some phrenology art, like using different offbeat occult systems to make a point. And you had a person's brain, and instead of the signs that were usually associated with phrenology you had Prince Albert Tobacco can coverings and apples, things like that. This was done in 1967?

BS: Yes.

IR: So you've been consistently interested in offbeat science. Like what we call astrology.

BS: Yes, like the occult arts.

IR: Yes, occult arts. When did you get interested in that? Have you always been interested in this?

BS: I've always been interested in it, but it never entered into my work graphically, I guess, until 1965, when I was into drawing zodiac signs and star charts and that led to palmistry and phrenology and then the phrenology went from the head of a phrenology chart to a man's head to a black man's head (facing page) and that evolved into the black thing. But even in the pieces that are the black pieces they still have some reflection back to the occult sciences, even to the star and the moon, which to me represents how the stars rule our lives, or destiny or fate or whatever. But I like a flashback from the tribal hangings to the black images to the occult sciences or to have them all in one.

IR: I went to the show twice. The first time I got a very superficial reading of the show. I was reading the show being—coming from another field, coming from another attitude—someone who has not developed his eye as well as an artist has. The more you look at

it the more you see. There are hidden elements in it. It will trick you. I'm sure if you went back every day, you'd have a thing where you go to see it thirty days or something and just take notes. What was so hip about this was most of the time people exhibit. The old idea of an exhibit is where you go to a museum and you look at the stuff and all the art is there. You did have some hidden pieces. Would you like to explain some of the stuff that the audience didn't see? The patrons didn't see? For example, what was in those vials?

BS: Oh! Well, the whole *Mojo* series or the tribal hangings, each one of those pieces has a secret, a secret root that only the person who buys it or the person I know knows about. And the piece you're speaking of now is called *Gris-Gris Box*. You open a panel and inside there are some little wooden boxes—little columns of wood—and you open them and inside each one is something that could be used for a gris-gris or to make a kind of magic thing. They are organic materials.

IR: Like what?

BS: Shells, bark from a tree, bones from a small bird, and pods. I don't know what that pod is—it rattles, it has a sound. Another thing I tried to do with the mojos, with the whole series, was to get into a sensitivity thing. Certain materials would have odor, like sandalwood, or carob pods have a distinct odor. They are also very tactile, like fur and leather, things to touch and things that make sounds, like pieces of wood or pods with seeds that would rattle or bones that would

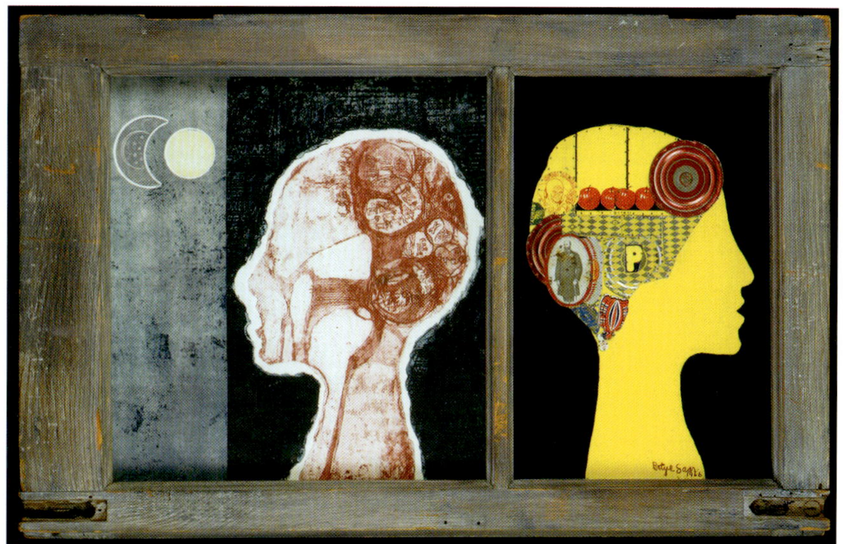

Betye Saar, *The Phrenologer's Window*, 1966. Mixed media assemblage, 18½ × 29¾ × 1 in. (47.0 × 75.6 × 2.5 cm). Courtesy of the artist and Roberts Projects, Los Angeles

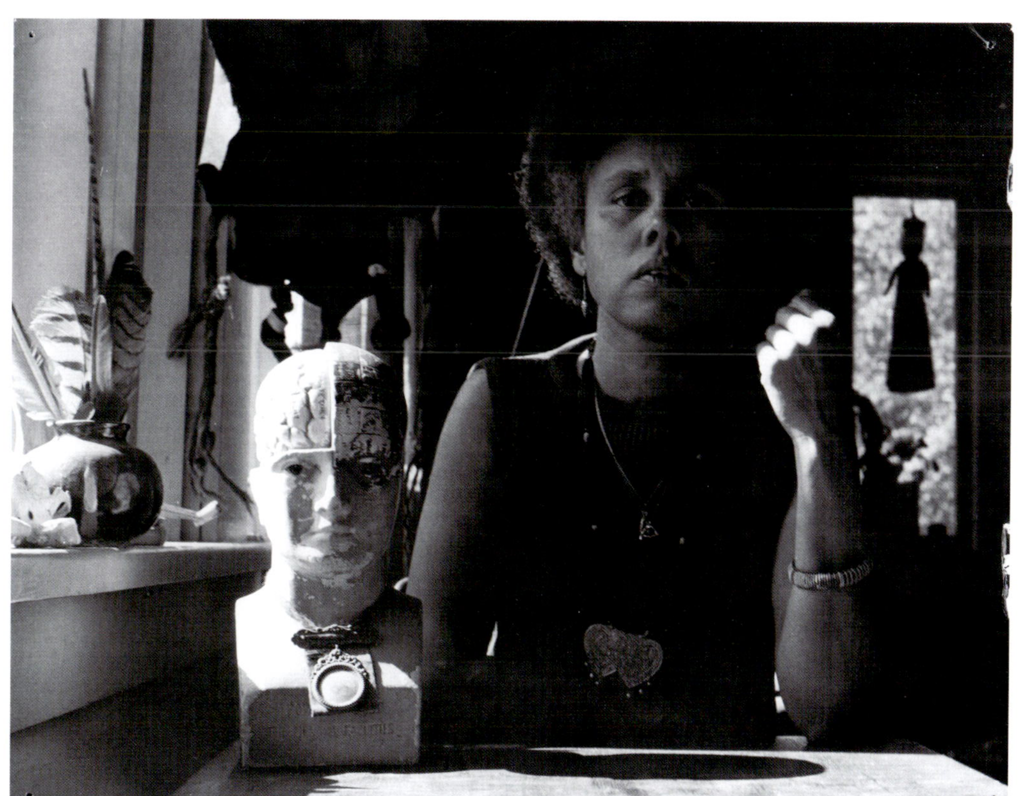

Betye Saar with her work in her Laurel Canyon residence, 1971. Courtesy of the artist and Roberts Projects, Los Angeles

     DRIFTING TOWARD TWILIGHT

rattle. So it would be more than just the sensitivity of sight. One would get into smell and sound.

IR: Incidentally, have you ever gotten into trouble with the ecology movement over those dead birds? (Joke.)

BS: No.

IR: You also like a lot of precious little things. *Stuff.*

BS: Stuff you're supposed to throw away.

IR: Well, but they look very big—they glisten—they look very good. What is some of the stuff that you have in there? I saw throughout the work like little bits and pieces of things—like marble, with all kind of jewelry effects and things. It looks so busy. What was that?

BS: Well, it's just like—I guess some of it could be junk, but I try not to collect junk. I like old things. Old things have secrets of where they've been before, people that they've related to. So I go to thrift shops and flea markets and things like that—some things people give to me, some things I just find. In a parking lot you can find little bits of tin or something that somebody's lost—and it's the way that they're put together that gives that jewel-like quality, because isolated it's just nothing. It's the way that they relate to each other. Certain things have a certain look about them that's enhanced by what they're placed next to.

IR: I was interested in one that seemed to stand out. Let me go into this other thing first. In Vodoun they have a thing called *gros-ben-age* which allows each individual to bequeath his essential qualities to the world. I guess it's kind of like your soul, the *ka* of a person. I was reminded of this when I saw that piece you did on your grandmother. And it was like everybody's grandmother. I was thinking of the petals and the old rusted photo and the idealized picture—I'm talking about *Grandma's Garden*, 1972—close to *Grandma's House* and in *Grandma's House* you had her glasses, all the lace, everything that you associate with that (p. 59). And it gave it a spiritual quality because the stuff you used in it was kind of like ghostly—the soul of Grandmotherhood.

BS: Like faded memory.

IR: Yeah, too much.

BS: The thing about *Grandma's Garden*—I was flashing back. Sometimes an artist has to see their work all out there to realize what they were really doing. And when I made that box I had these dried petals and dried flowers and this old photo of two ladies in this garden and this piece of sheet music that said "My Garden of Memory" and then the butterflies. But when I put the petals down I found little beads and little pieces of glass and I glued those in. Because when I was a child my grandmother had this house at 117th Street, in Watts, and I would spend my summers there. And I would be in the yard digging with a stick all the time. And I would find little pieces of glass and beads, and it would be like pulling up weeds, and there would be some little thing that would be like a treasure to me.

To a five-year-old kid it's a treasure. And I think that's where I became a junky, that's where I started collecting that stuff, because I would always go home with a bunch of that stuff.

IR: So as not to be misunderstood, you weren't collecting heroin, you were collecting these little pieces. . . .

BS: Yeah, junk—like junk.

IR: Junky.

BS: Right, right. Well, that's my own inside joke. But that's what my studio's like. It's like, it's filled with stuff, junk—junk, but when I put it all together—when I made that *Grandma's Garden*, to make that I had to hide those things because those were the things that I found. But not everybody sees that. I have to point that out—that's another secret.

IR: There's one piece that really stands out. From this show, like a sore thumb. What piece am I going to talk about?

BS: From what series?

IR: It's called the *Vision of Cremo*, 1967, in which you have a figure from Greek mythology—Pegasus. And it's not a red horse—it's a green horse this time, and there's a fisherman thing there. A green horse.

BS: Oh, that Pegasus thing. That actually is something that I found and I didn't think of Pegasus when I put it in. Remember, there used to be a gas station called Flying A?

IR: Yeah.

BS: That was the symbol there. See at that particular time I was working [in] a stream of consciousness where there was no direction. That just like took over—I'm not going to say that I was possessed or anything like that. But things just fit in.

IR: It's like looking for the well with the witch's stick where you go all over the place until you find the well.

BS: Right, right, right—it's that kind of thing. So that piece kind of evolved that way. I'm still trying to figure out why I use things like that—those pieces in that one. Sometimes I know exactly what I'm doing, but a lot of times. . . .

IR: I'll bet'ya I know. . . .

BS: You do?

IR: I'll think about it more though—I think I can read the artist reading the show. Not in a Freudian sense, but trying to use all the knowledge available. You do draw from many cultures, like there was a Chicano piece called *Fiesta of the Dead* (p. 32). Where did that come from?

BS: The idea comes from the basic piece. And that was like a wooden tray of early California. I based the thing on that. It has a horseman in it . . . that horseman could mean time passing or whatever—and then sometimes I just have a feeling, like there's a dancing couple in it—I guess that's to indicate music or whatever to make the

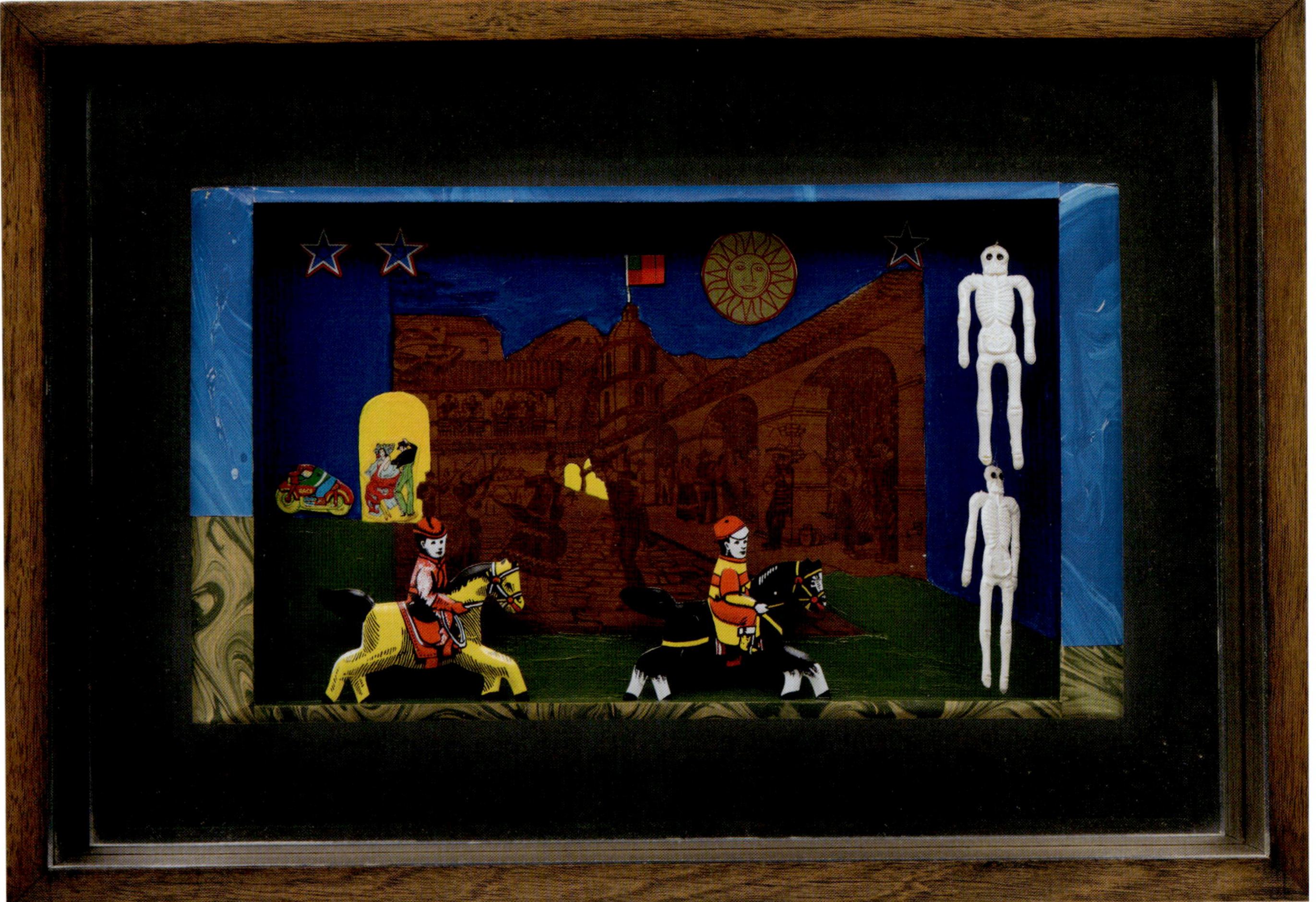

Betye Saar, *Fiesta of the Dead*, 1969. Mixed media assemblage, 9¾ × 14½ × 1¾ in. (24.8 × 36.8 × 4.4 cm). Courtesy of the artist and Roberts Projects, Los Angeles

fiesta kind of thing. But then also they have that fiesta, Los Muertos or something like that, with the skulls and skeletons. . . .

IR: That's another recurrent element in your work—skeletons.

BS: Right, right. Which is death, because death is part of life.

IR: I'm glad you told me. . . .

BS: No—or it could be Halloween, or it could be anything. That's why I use that.

IR: I want to get back to why you use what people popularly call "Third World" materials and subject. But *Lama*, 1972, in which you used these ivory pieces, these dice-like objects with ancient characters on them—were they done at any particular time in connection with your new ideas, or—how did they come in there? Do you work on a series of work and all of a sudden an alien idea comes in and you go to that and then come back? How does that work?

BS: Well, if it's all in your head, how can it be an alien idea?

BETYE SAAR

IR: I mean alien to the project you're working on.

BS: But the head is always working on projects. But I know what you mean. That particular work is the work that I really enjoy doing. That one, *Lama*, *The Essence of Egypt*, and *Wizard* are three of a series where I deal with the mystical philosophies or secret societies of other groups.

IR: I saw the one of the men with the white paint—white body paint on them!

BS: Oh, that's in the mojo, *Ten Mojo Secrets*—that's another secret. I'm talking about those little boxes—that was a special series, secret societies, like the *Tibetan Book of the Dead*, like what that involves with *Lama* and those ivory squares are from a mojo—everything is like common things, but when they're put together, they get into a special thing. So that's a lama meditating with his particular secret society.

IR: A critic saw your show, and he described it as explaining why black people are angry and bitter. What would you think of that assessment?

BS: Well, it's something that I have said that comes from those derogatory images, even though they aren't particularly used during our time, like today, because most of those things have been destroyed or put back. But it's like if it happened in your father's time or your grandfather's time, those hurts are still passed down to you, and it's just kind of one way of explaining why the anger is still within the black man—

it's because of all that other stuff that happened before and those images are part of that. They're just comical graphic things—it's not the real thing except for the lynchings. Those are the photographs of the real thing.

IR: Your show has been very well received, critically. How did you think the criticism ran? Did you think the criticism was very bright or was it intelligent or . . . ?

BS: No, because it was just based on things I said. There was one review in *Artweek* where the woman really looked at the work. . . .

IR: What was the woman's name?

BS: Lynn Hershman. She reviewed the work and compared it with other artists who worked in the same technique.

IR: Like who?

BS: Joseph Cornell and . . .

IR: Arthur Dove.

BS: Yeah, and to me her review was more meaningful because she departed from my own statement about my work. You read four other reviews, and there are certain things that are said in each one of them, which meant that either the man wasn't thinking or he was lazy when he was writing it.

IR: I was at a conference, and a gentleman said—I was proposing that some of these cultural organizations use their foundation money to open up gallery exchanges that would deal [in] Afro-American artists, that would promote them and guarantee gallery space all over the country—and the gentleman said that some of the Afro-American artists were doing things that the "community" couldn't relate to, and he thought that what they should really be doing are like charcoals. What do you think about that kind of statement?

BS: Well, he has limited vision because he evidently hasn't seen what's going on. True, there are some artists who do things that "the public" or "the community" couldn't accept, but there are just as many artists doing other things. "The community" hasn't seen—particularly "this community" hasn't seen—the kind of thing that I've done until I had it up there. So I didn't know whether they would accept it or reject it. You have to take a chance.

IR: We've gone through ten years or so—these have been years of people finding their racial identity in an era of black pride and many symbols like the clenched fist have arisen. I was reading where the national income of blacks in this country is up to forty billion dollars, so with all this enthusiasm for racial pride and all this I'm sure blacks are flocking to buy the works of Afro-American painters. In your discussions with other painters do you find that this is what's happening?

BS: No. Now, with my particular pieces I try to keep the prices so that people who really like them will buy them. Of course, they're not always shown where people with money [can] come. But I know of several collectors who think it's more of an investment to buy white art. I understand a certain famous black athlete has a big million-dollar house and it's filled with non-black art. . . .

IR: What does he have in his house?

BS: I've never been there. All I know is some artists who say he hasn't bought black art. And they're black artists.

IR: I hope he's careful about what he buys. There's a reattribution thing going on in the Metropolitan—they're finding fakes all over the place. Well, not really fakes, but [work] attributed to people like Goya, and they were done by Goya's brother or the dog—Goya's dog or the gardener.

BS: Right, right. Well, a lot of those people had apprentices who painted in their style.

IR: So this really, like Vietnam, collapsed, and now the Watergate. When they talk about standards they don't really know what standards are. This scandal is kind of the equivalent to a tuberculosis outbreak—a political, economic, and cultural epidemic, you know. Sophy Burnham wrote a book called *The Art Crowd*, showing the Watergates in the art world run by people who think they are superior to Nixon.

BS: Well, it's time for a new art scandal.

IR: But I mean, they say that Afro-Americans don't have standards. I'm talking about this reattribution thing—what does it say about Western standards?

BS: But all Western art is based on African art.

IR: Would you go into that—like all of it?

BS: It's based on, let's say, non-European art because it's either Asian or African or Egyptian. Like there was a book sold during the time of the Olympic Games. A great amount of study had been gone into where they compared contemporary European artists and where they got their technique. For instance, everyone knows Picasso was doing landscapes and portraits until he saw some African art. Of course, you see you really need an art historian to go into that. Because I'm not going to lie and make a comparison because I'm into doing it, not comparing it.

IR: When did you become interested in being an artist?

BS: I picked up a sketchbook that I made in 1942—funny little sketches. So I know I was doing it then. And then I have also drawings from when I was in kindergarten. So I was always into art and drawing and my mother was interested in art, and she always encouraged me to take special art classes and things like that. However, it wasn't until maybe '60, '62 when I decided that I was an artist. Before then I was like a designer or a craftsman or something else like that.

IR: So you've had a very successful show here in Berkeley Live Oak Park Gallery. So what's up ahead? Next?

BS: This exhibit goes in part to Humboldt State College and part to the Los Angeles County Museum of Art. And to other small shows and galleries and places where I've been invited to participate.

IR: You've also been lecturing. You went to Oberlin College? How was it there? How did you like it?

BS: Oh, that was nice. I like that because I'd do a slide presentation which allowed the students to see what I am doing. And I just talk about my work and what I think about when I do it. And how I do it. And I usually just relate to whatever questions they ask me—you know—whatever feedback I get. What materials I use or whatever they come from—that's what I extend from. The direction that my art is taking (as well as the graphic things that are in the gallery) is filmmaking, because I'm interested in films about my art, an extension—like you see a piece, you look at a window and there's a picture of a sun or a face or a skeleton. So from that I would go to all things that relate to that kind of image. Other astrology signs or whatever. It would be like a kind of animated thing, but it's just like film is art.

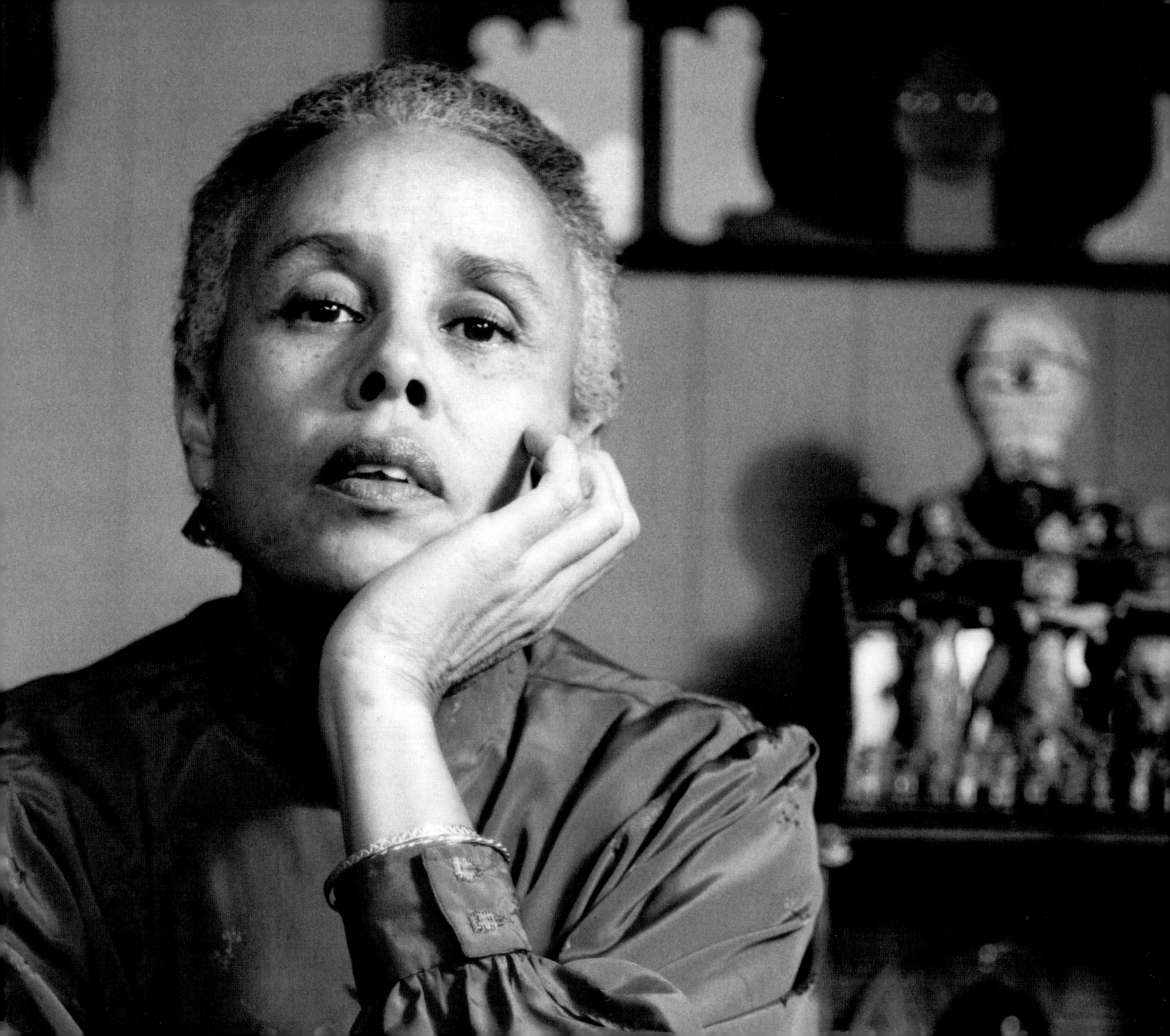

HILTON ALS

BETYE SAAR REASSEMBLES THE LIVES OF BLACK WOMEN

The artist Betye Saar lives less than two miles from the bars, billboards, and bustle of Los Angeles's Sunset Boulevard, but her home, in Laurel Canyon, seems far removed from Sunset's gleaming capitalism and packaged sex. Saar's studio and house, where she has lived for more than sixty years—she is now ninety-seven— are dedicated to history, especially American history as it relates to Black women. In her work, that history is often told through pop-culture artifacts, which, in Saar's hands, take on a witty poetic resonance—an aura—that they wouldn't otherwise have. Just as Jasper Johns used the flag and beer cans to critique our ideas of the sacred and the disposable, Saar uses objects to address the power of the image in America. But her America is to the left of Johns's largely male-oriented world. Her layered assemblages, which sometimes resemble the interior of a hope chest, are also filled with inquiry: into the nature of mythology, and specifically how and why we mythologize the Black woman.

Saar uses prefabricated pieces (Black dolls, Aunt Jemima paraphernalia, advertising images, and the like) to show us how women of color have been repeatedly treated as props—accommodating, beneficent

characters—in the never-ending drama of race. These images rarely even hint at an interior life, but Saar makes that interiority manifest. Her seminal work, *The Liberation of Aunt Jemima* (1972)—which the activist Angela Davis reportedly credited with sparking the Black women's movement—is a box containing a smiling Mammy figure with a gun under her arm, ready to blow all those stereotypes away (p. 38). In the installation work *A Loss of Innocence* (1998), Saar suspends a long white cotton and lace dress from a hanger above a child-size wooden chair; to the bottom of the gown she has attached labels with words such as *Pickaninny*, *Tar Baby*, and *Coon Baby*—epithets that not only besmirch innocence but remove the very possibility of it. What are children of color left with? The sense that no one, not even a loving parent, can protect them from a world of hate. Saar's white dress, which looks homemade, brings to mind another frequent theme: women's labor as a locus of creative ingenuity. Washtubs, jewelry boxes, sewing materials, buttons, and ribbons all appear in her art: she wants us to see how the world is constructed by the hands of invisible women who make it *work*.

Betye Saar, 1978. Courtesy of the artist and Roberts Projects, Los Angeles

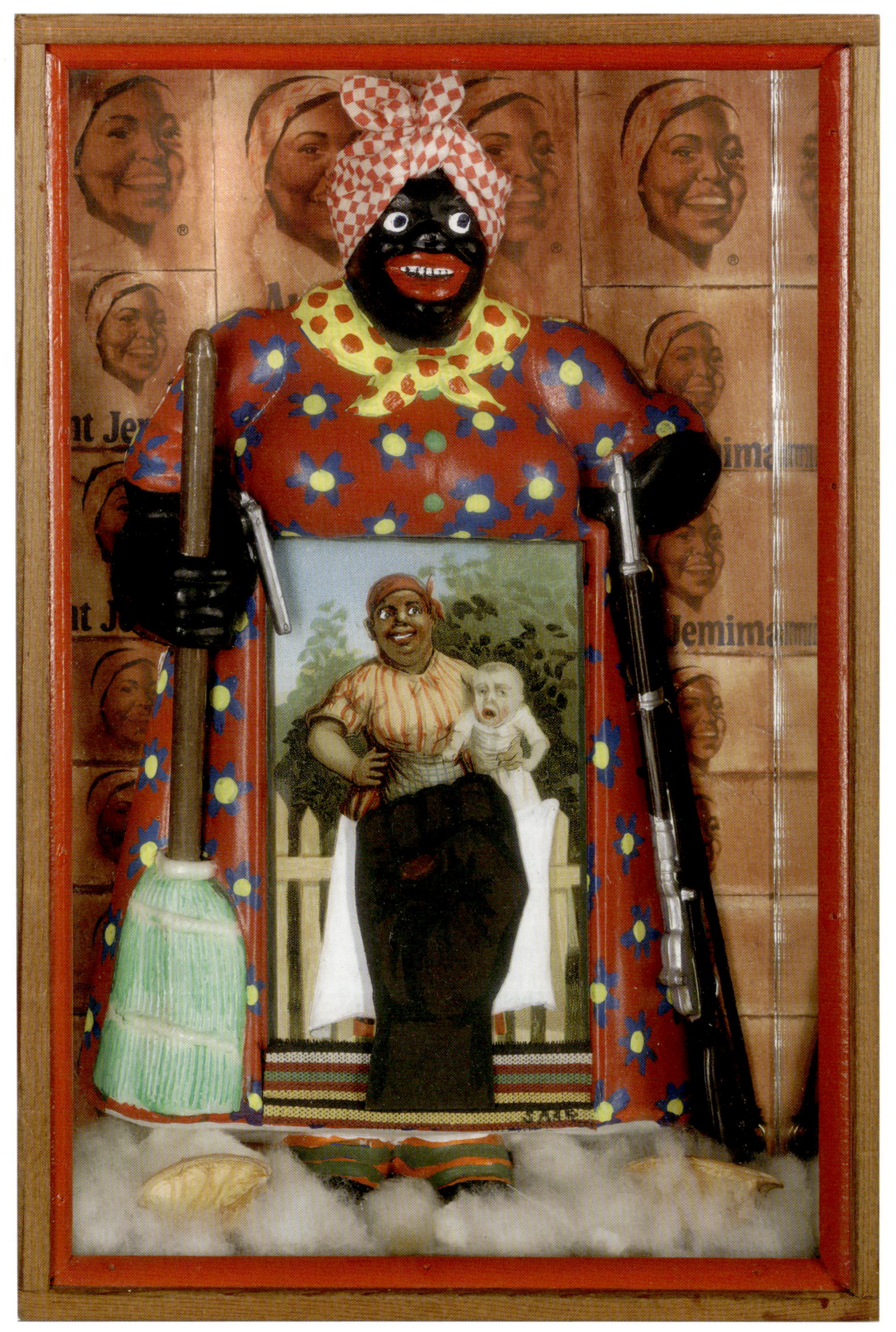

Betye Saar, *The Liberation of Aunt Jemima*, 1972. Mixed media assemblage, 11¾ × 8 × 2¾ in. (29.9 × 20.3 × 7.0 cm). Berkeley Art Museum and Pacific Film Archive, Berkeley, California; Purchased with the aid of funds from the National Endowment for the Arts (selected by The Committee for the Acquisition of Afro-American Art). Courtesy of the artist and Roberts Projects, Los Angeles

BETYE SAAR

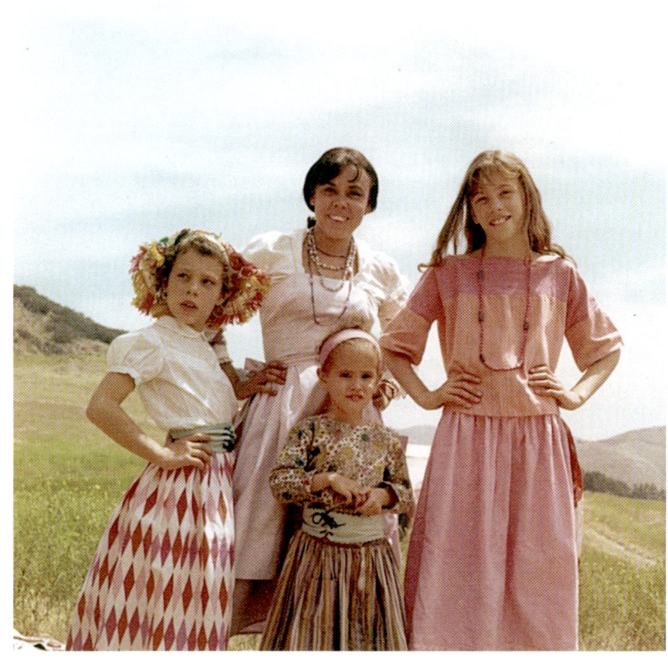

Alison, Betye, Tracye, and Lezley Saar at the Renaissance Pleasure Faire, at Paramount Ranch in Agoura Hills, California, 1965. Courtesy of the artist and Roberts Projects, Los Angeles

Behind a pink door in Saar's house, above her studio, is a small kitchen; opposite the stove and the counter, she has fashioned a sitting area. The space is snug; the windows look out onto the trees and foliage of Laurel Canyon. You have the sense of gazing down from the deck of a great ship. In both the kitchen and the sitting area there are ceramic Aunt Jemima–like figures, cloth dolls in brightly colored skirts, clocks, and any number of other elements that you might see in a Betye Saar assemblage. The artist herself— dressed, on the afternoon that I saw her, in February, in loose gray pants, a gray T-shirt, and an oversize plaid shirt—is small, too, but age has done little to diminish the magnitude of thought and feeling in her eyes when she speaks, in a voice that is light, youthful, and mischievous.

Saar moved to this house in 1962 with her then husband, the ceramicist Richard Saar—they divorced in 1970, but remained close until his death, in 2004. ("Are you married?" she asked me. "It's a *job*.") Laurel Canyon was "a hippie place" then, according to Saar, one where an interracial couple—Richard was white—and their three daughters, Lezley, Alison, and Tracye, were unlikely to be hassled. Frank Zappa lived nearby, and the canyon was still fairly rustic. It was a place where Saar, who had grown up not knowing that a Black woman could be an artist, began to find her creative footing. The energy of second-wave feminism and the rush of Black nationalist politics helped.

★ ● ★

Saar believes in the importance of the psychic world not only in art but in life, because she has lived in it. Born in Los Angeles in 1926, she was the eldest child of Jefferson Maze Brown and Beatrice Lillian Parson, who moved to California, from Louisiana and Missouri, respectively, to study at UCLA. Both parents had great respect for education, and pushed Saar and her two younger siblings to embrace its possibilities. But even as a little girl, Saar had another life that was separate from the family's, one that she has tried to make visible in her work. "As a child, I was clairvoyant," she told me. "I remember living in a particular house. I was maybe four years old, and would play in the carriage house in the back yard. There I imagined a friend named Rosie, who was always telling me stories. I'd come into the house and say, 'Rosie says that Dad's going to be late from work today because he missed his bus.' And then my dad would come in later. He'd say, 'Oh, honey, I missed the bus.' And my mother would say, 'Oh, yeah, Betye told us that.'" Shortly after

DRIFTING TOWARD TWILIGHT

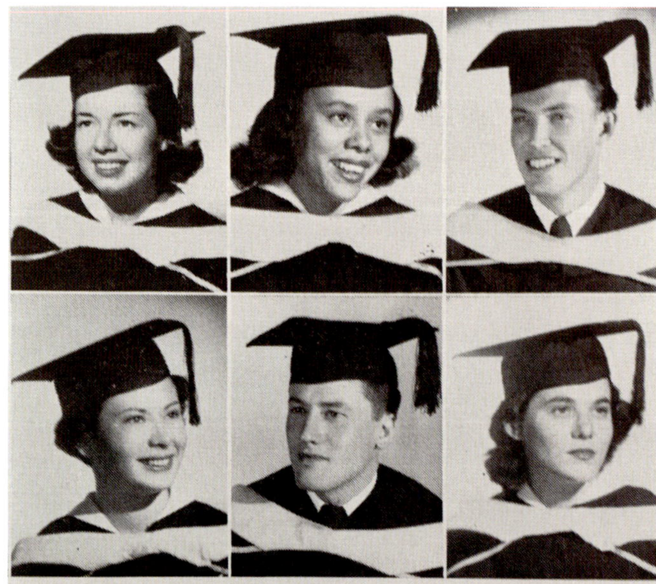

Alma Eloise Brown; A.B.; Political Science; Los Angeles; Class council 1, 2, 3, 4; OCB 1, 2; **Scop** Publicity director 3, 4; Tropicana, 2, 3.

Betty Irene Brown; A.B.; Interior Decoration; Pasadena; Transfer: Pasadena city college; ΑΚΑ; ΔΕ.

Jack Herbert Brown; B.S.; Marketing; Glendale; Transfer: University of Idaho; ΣΑΕ; All-U-Sing Exec. bd.; Council, 3; Editor, **Claw**.

Carol Irene Bruns; A.B.; Political Science; Springfield, Illinois; ΚΔ; International Relations club; Class Council 1, 2, 3, 4.

Edward Walter Buchanan Jr.; B.S.; Physical Ed.; Darien, Connecticut; Transfer: University of Georgia; ΤΚΕ; Council 1,2; Soccer; Diving.

Marilyn Buchanan; A.B.; Sociology; Riverside; Transfer: Riverside city college.

Saar turned five, her father died of an infection, and Rosie died with him. Still, Saar's early experience—and her parents' support—gave her the assurance to trust her vision and her imagination.

After Brown's death, the family lived first with his mother in Watts and then in Pasadena, where Beatrice supported her children by working at a department store and as a seamstress. Saar, a child of the Depression, also sewed from a young age, and made trinkets that she sold to her playmates and their families. After high school, Saar wanted to study art, but art schools at that time were largely segregated. "The Chouinard Art Institute was available to me, but it was private," Saar wrote in a 2016 essay in *Frieze*. "And that was just one of the things black people didn't go into—they didn't study to be artists." Fine art was for white people who came from a different class—one in which art could be a vocation. If you were Black, you had to find a job, some stability in an unstable world. Saar's stepfather—her mother remarried when she was eleven—asked her, "Now, what are you studying art for? How are you going to make any money like that?" Saar told me. "And I said, 'I suppose there are designers. They design cars. They design clothes. I can just be a designer.'" So Saar took design-related classes at Pasadena City College for two years, before transferring to UCLA, thanks to an organization that raised money to pay tuition for minority students. There, she studied applied arts. "I didn't take fine-art classes," she said. "In fact, I think I was afraid of painting—thinking, You really have to be an artist to paint."

After graduating, in 1949, Saar found employment as a social worker. The poverty and desperation she witnessed left a mark on her consciousness. Her face still fills with compassionate sadness when she remembers that job. "To have no resources, to be a woman with no resources . . . ," she said, then fell silent. Around the same time, she and her friend the jewelry designer and painter Curtis Tann launched a small business, Brown and Tann, selling enamel jewelry, bowls, and plates that they had designed (see p. 90). Tann introduced her to other Black artists, including Charles White, who believed that Black art could be as much about racial uplift as it was about the artist's aesthetics.

The lessons Saar had learned from her parents about the importance of education and work—who were you if you weren't striving?—kept her on the move. In 1958, she began graduate studies at California State University, Long Beach, where she discovered printmaking. She was on campus one day when she smelled something strange. It was ink: "I wandered into the printmaking studio, and they were making all these things, and putting them in the presses and all. I said, 'I want to learn to do that.'" To hear Saar describe the technical aspects of printmaking—"I had so much fun doing something which is called a 'soft ground'; that's putting an oily substance, like a grease, on a piece of metal, and drawing through to the metal. Then you put it in the acid. The grease resists the acid"—is to witness an enthusiast who believes in the joyful *how* of making the imagination visible.

✶ ● ✶

"What can you do?" she said. We were sitting at her kitchen table, talking about how the death of Martin Luther King Jr., in 1968, had prompted a more political voice in her work. "You're a young mother—you can't go to marches. You have to stay home and take care of your kids. You could contribute. I didn't have a lot of money. So, what could I do to express that?" Her answer was her art. By then, all of Saar's skills—as a printmaker, a designer, and a seamstress—had coalesced, in part because she'd found another artist whose vocabulary made sense to her. In early 1967, she visited the Pasadena Art Museum and discovered an exhibition of work by the brilliant assemblage artist Joseph Cornell (p. 42). Saar was exhilarated by the worlds that Cornell created in boxes: unapologetically romantic and history-rich cosmoses, where dreams and cultural artifacts and even the stars Cornell loved, ranging from Lauren Bacall to Susan Sontag, were presented as though on a stage. The boxes, filled with images torn from magazines, old postcards evocative of a cultured Europe, fragments from old manuscripts, dolls, taxidermy birds, and so on, had a galvanizing effect on Saar. She soon began collecting materials to make assemblages of her own.

One of the things Saar found touching about Cornell was that some of his works were made to amuse his brother, Robert, who had cerebral palsy. Saar wanted her art to have a "healing effect," too. I asked if she wanted to redeem people with her work. "Yeah. But not to preach, not to control. To give them a hint that there's something else. There's always *other*. And if you open yourself up to *other*, you can do and think all sorts of things."

Among the first significant pieces Saar made was *Black Girl's Window* (1969) (see p. 26). A deeply personal work, it is a mixed media assemblage that, like a Cornell, is contained in a wooden box—its "frame." In it there are nine small panels, or windows, above a larger one. Two contain a quarter moon; another, an array of sun and stars. There's a skeleton, a roaring lion—Saar is a Leo—and a daguerreotype of a white woman, a reference to Saar's maternal grandmother, who was Irish. But the most significant figure in the

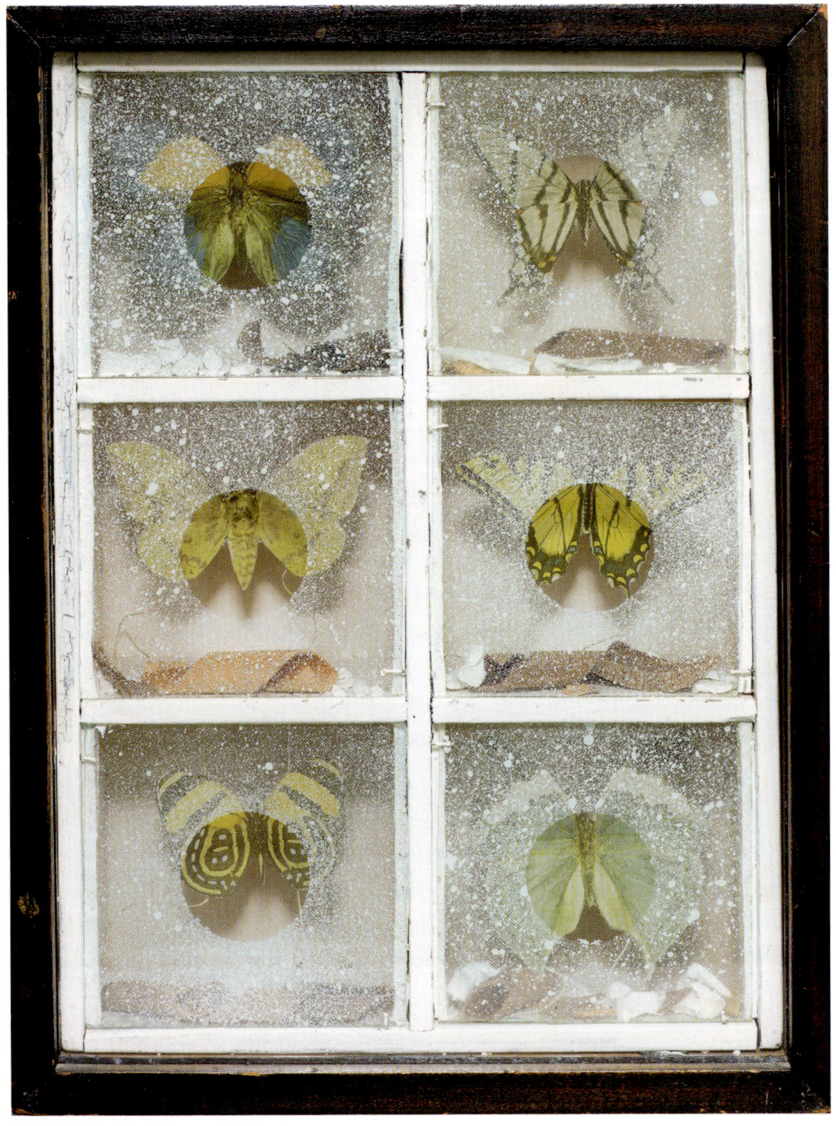

Joseph Cornell, *Untitled (Butterfly Habitat)*, ca. 1940. Box construction with painted glass, 12 × 9⅛ × 3⅛ in. (30.5 × 23.2 × 8.0 cm). Art Institute of Chicago, Lindy and Edwin Bergman Joseph Cornell Collection, 1982.1845

piece is a Black woman. She is seen in silhouette at the bottom of the frame, her eyes her only visible feature. Her hands are held up and pressed against the glass that contains her; her fingers glitter with moons, stars, and astrological symbols. The Black woman is looking out at us—a kind of forceful looking. We are welcome to look at her, too, but we're not allowed inside: this is her world, her life, and it's dense with waking dreams and possibilities.

Saar's breakthrough works couldn't have come at a better time. Los Angeles was waking up to its Black artists. In 1967, two brothers, Alonzo Davis and Dale Brockman Davis, founded the Brockman Gallery, which featured Black and other minority artists. The following year, the great painter Suzanne Jackson opened Gallery 32, where she showed works by the then relatively unknown David Hammons, the visual poet Senga Nengudi, and Saar. Artists moved between the two galleries; this was more about community than capital, and community bonds were strengthened by the era's many upheavals: the Watts rebellion, the radicalism of the Black Panther Party. The escalation of violence and racial injustice made Saar want to push back. *The Liberation of Aunt Jemima* did just that. As Saar says, it changed "a person of servitude to a soldier, to a fighter. Fighting for political rights. For personal rights." She calls *Aunt Jemima* her first politically explicit work, but I would argue that it wasn't. In the designs she created for Brown and Tann and in her early assemblages, there is already an awareness of what it means to look out at a world that looks back at you with its own twisted vision. The Mammy figure is, of course, a distortion of the Black female body. (The scholar Patricia A. Turner has described racist dolls and figurines like the ones that Saar uses in her work as "contemptible collect-ibles.") Saar worried, at first, about how the work would be perceived by a white audience and how that might influence "the ways in which Black people saw each other." She added, "What saved it was that I made Aunt Jemima into a revolutionary figure."

As her work began to attract notice in the 1970s and 1980s, Saar was able to travel more. She was drawn to the spirituality of objects created in parts of the Caribbean and Africa—drawn especially to cultures where the value of what you could not see (like her early experience with Rosie) was considered equal to that of what you could. It turned out that she had been doing similar work—spiritual and aesthetic work—all along. After reading the art historian Arnold Rubin's 1975 *Artforum* article "Accumulation: Power and Dis-play in African Sculpture," Saar understood even more fully why she constructed her assemblages in the way that she did. "He talked about how certain materials in African art have power and other materials are just for display or to help reinforce that power. That was a strong influence on me," she wrote in *Frieze*. "If you're making an assemblage, there's power in a certain part of the piece and then all the rest is decoration, either to throw off the negativity or to attract positive feel-ings. That's how I felt about my boxes or collages: the sacred element is located in a particular place in the composition." One could say the same about the

Black female body in Saar's work: the sacred element is the heart.

In the mid-1970s, Saar began incorporating into her work objects once owned by her great-aunt Hattie, who died in 1975. To look at pieces such as *Last Dance* (1975), which features items Hattie might have used for an evening out—a fan, a feather, a hair ribbon—or collages, such as *Letters from Home . . . Wish You Were Here* (1976) or *Night Letter: Some Day Some Place* (1977), that include missives penned by Hattie, is to feel oneself suspended between two forces: the dense, powerful weight of what a person leaves behind, and the melancholy understanding of how much honesty and artifice go into making a self. Are we true to our-selves as we become ourselves? Or are we impostors in our own lives?

In 1974, Saar recalls, she approached Marcia Tucker, then a curator at the Whitney Museum, after a talk Tucker gave in L.A. Tucker went to see Saar's work, and soon mounted a solo show at the Whitney. All Saar's years of work and creativity came together at a time when the art world was finally ready for her. Saar's 3-D combination of domestic realism and femi-nist dreams dovetailed with what many critics, includ-ing Lucy Lippard, saw happening then. "I thought serious artists had to have big, professional-looking spaces," Lippard wrote. "I found women in corners of men's studios, in bedrooms and children's rooms, even in kitchens, working away." Saar brought wom-en's lives and home life—the kitchen, the vanity table, the children's chairs—into gallery spaces.

Despite the critical support Saar has received, she has avoided the smug complacency that a lot of heralded artists sink into: *People love me, why should I try something different? Give 'em what they want.* She may use certain motifs again and again, but the underlying ethos of her work has to do with disposability and with change. Saar knows that the discarded, lost, and found things she uses in her work carry the full burden of our mortality, and the sweet wish that sometimes, against all odds, we can leave a lasting mark on others.

In November 2023, The Huntington unveiled Saar's latest large-scale piece, *Drifting Toward Twilight*. At the entrance to the blue-walled room where the installation is housed is a poem by Saar that reads, "The moon keeps vigil as a lone canoe drifts in a sea of tranquility seeking serenity in the twilight" (see p. 55). In times of war, both permanence and transience—the things that stay, and the things that we let go of in order to escape or survive—can have special resonance. This is certainly true of the seventeen-foot canoe at the center of this work, which was built in Maine during the Second World War. Resting on a bed of branches and vegetation, culled from the Huntington Botanical Gardens (which Saar visited on special occasions as a child), and filled with found objects—chairs, birdcages, antlers—the canoe speaks of journeys past and future.

The journey that Saar takes us on with this work has to do first with shape. We appreciate the sheer formal beauty of the canoe, the upward sweep of its stern and the curve of the bow. Before long, though, the object begins to move in our minds, carried along on the waves of history and myth: Charon ferrying dead souls across the River Styx; enslaved men in Brazil setting off in dugouts to fish; Vietnamese boat people; Syrian refugees landing in Greece but finding no home there, only the misery of refugee camps. Even out of such horror, Saar implies, beauty can be born.

Before I left Saar's home, I was able to see one of her workspaces, just off the kitchen. During the pandemic, she had begun to focus on watercolors, and her small paintings were vibrant and complete in the way that a child's can be: I couldn't imagine them being anything other than themselves. Did these paintings make her, at last, a "real artist"? I asked. "Until I get bored with this!" she said, smiling. Maybe the paintings would stay as they were; maybe they'd end up part of an assemblage or a collage. What was important to Saar were the times she was living in and their possibilities. "You can make art out of anything," she said.

PLATES

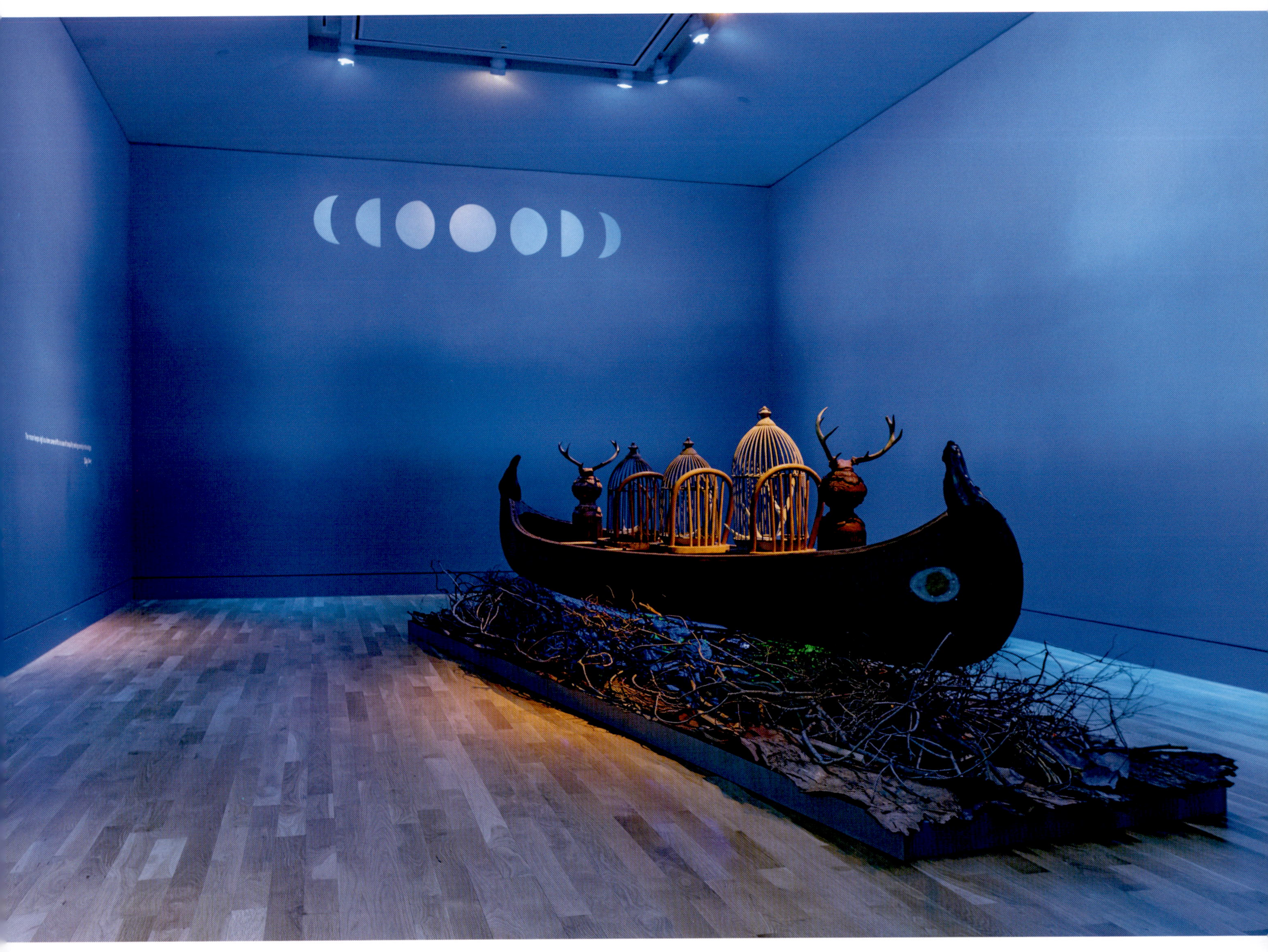

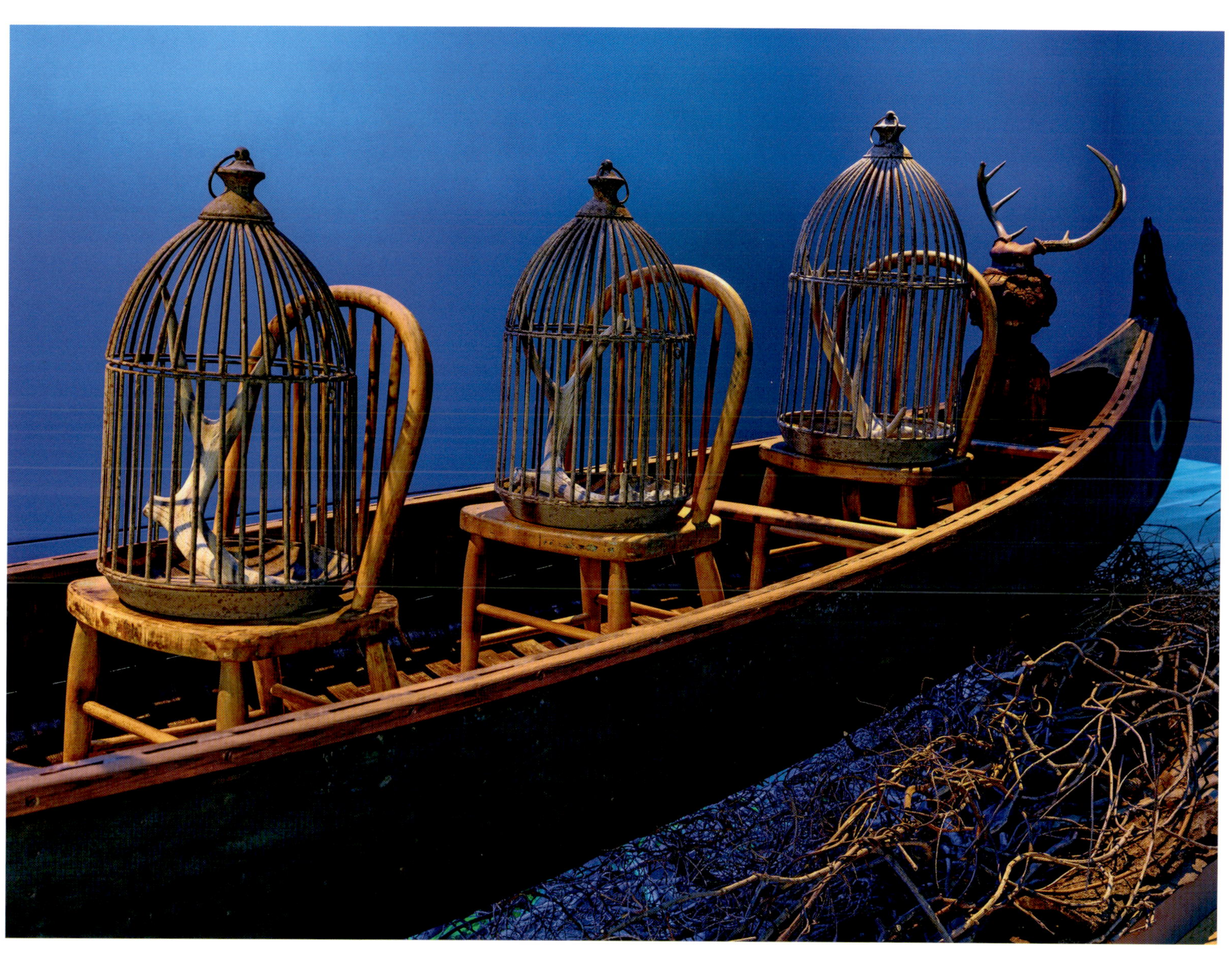

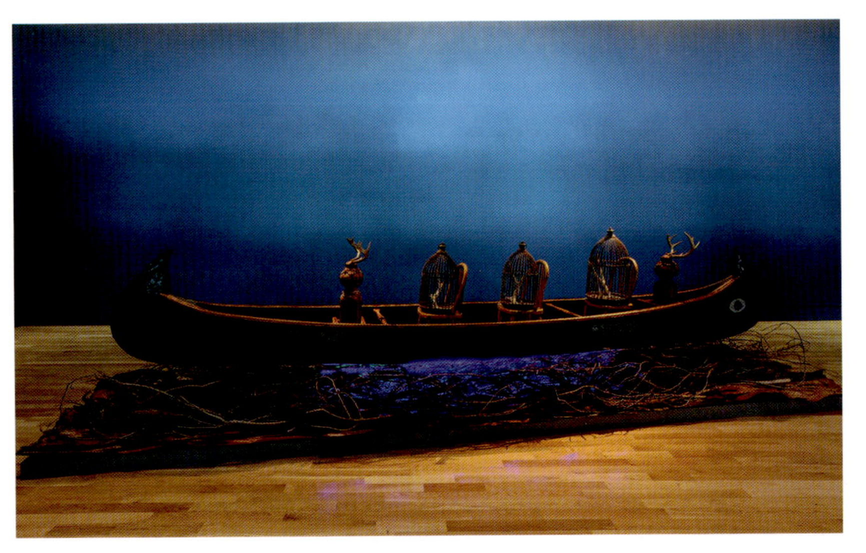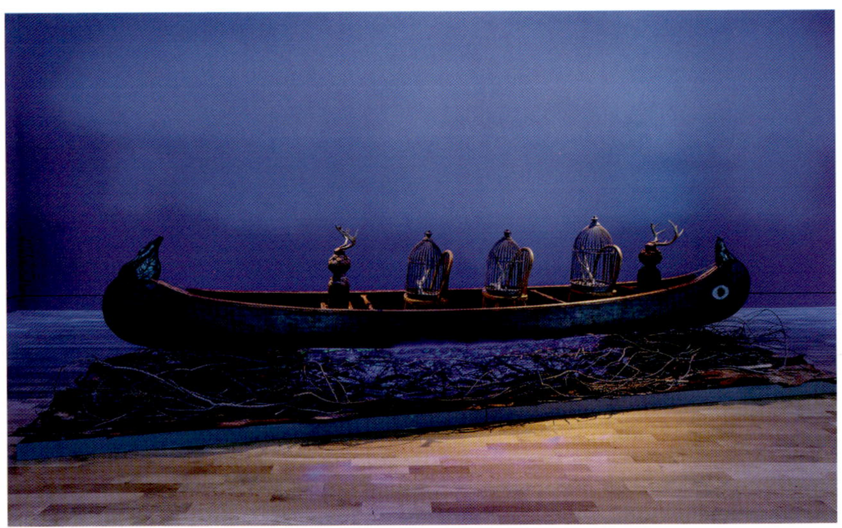

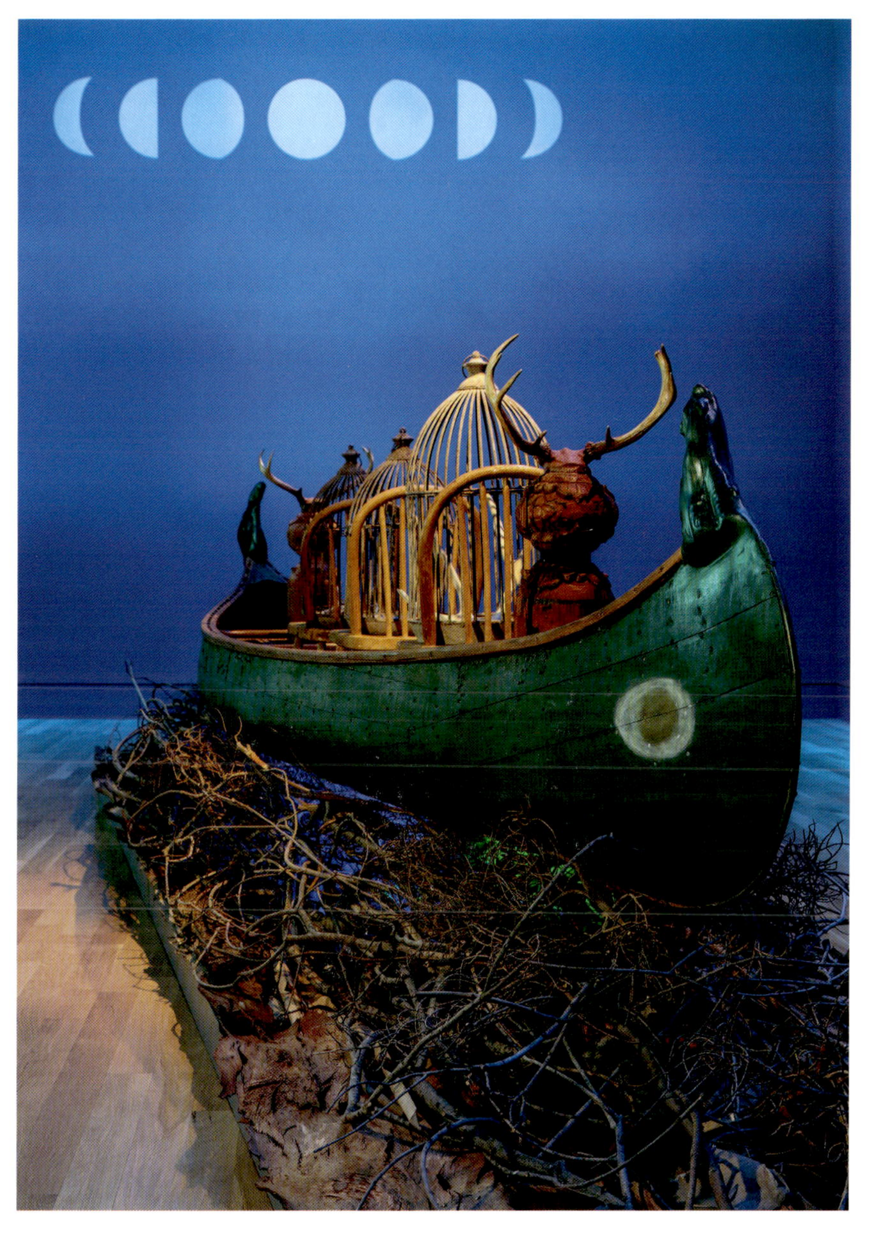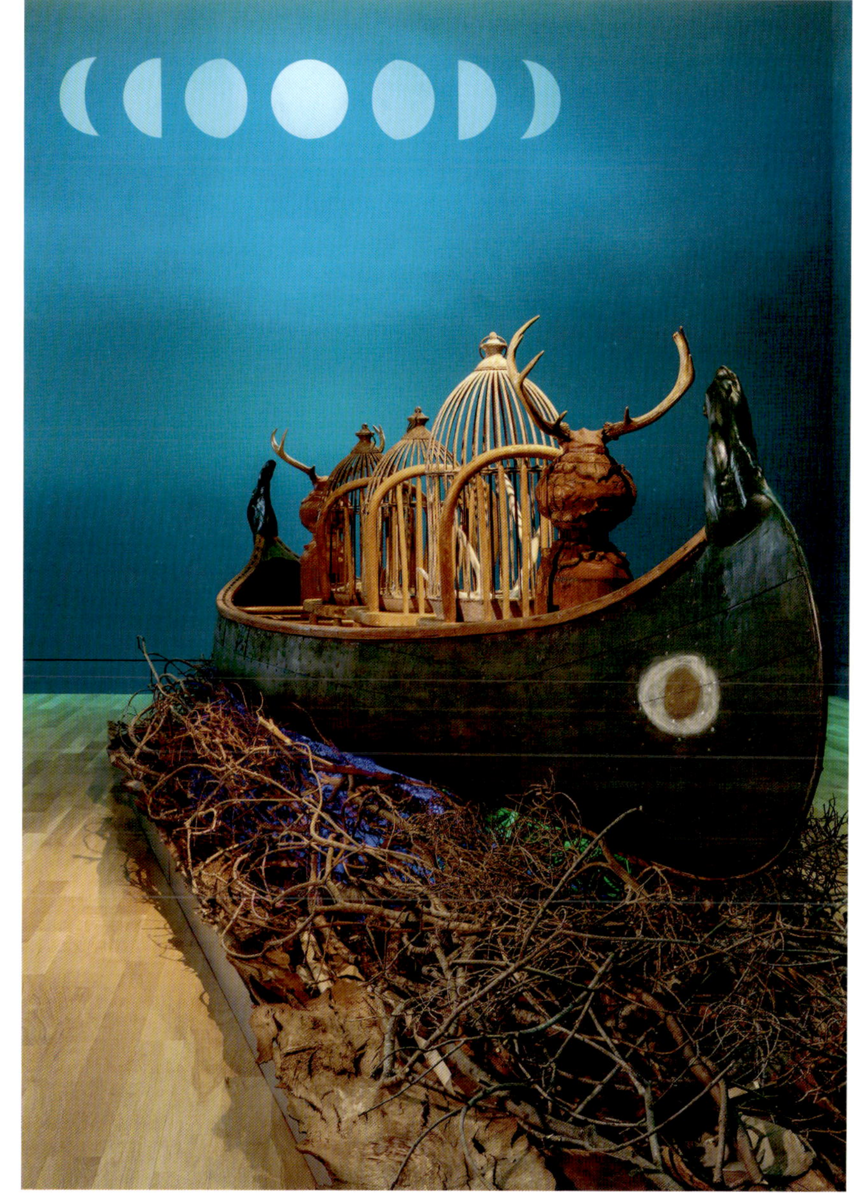

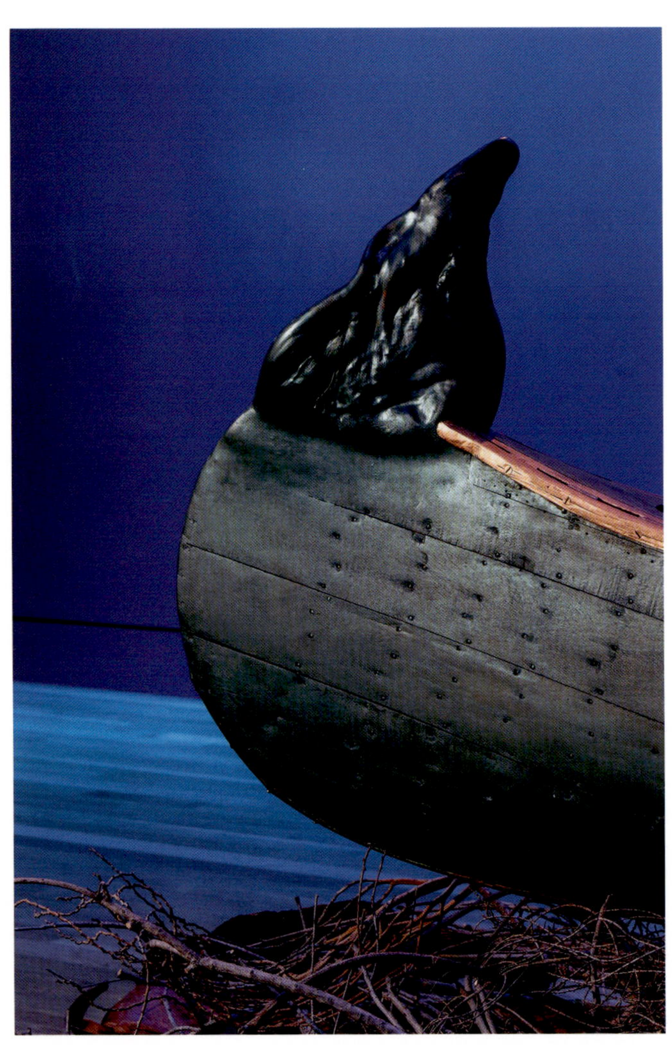
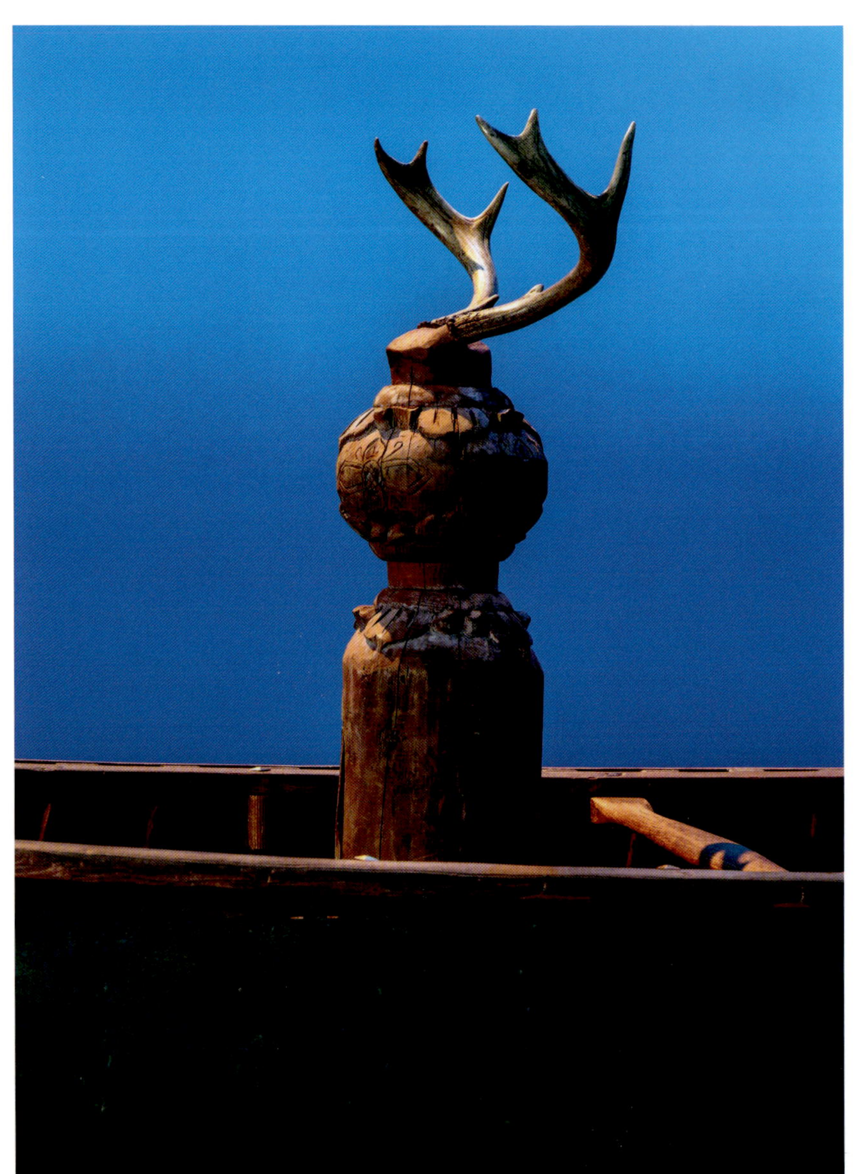

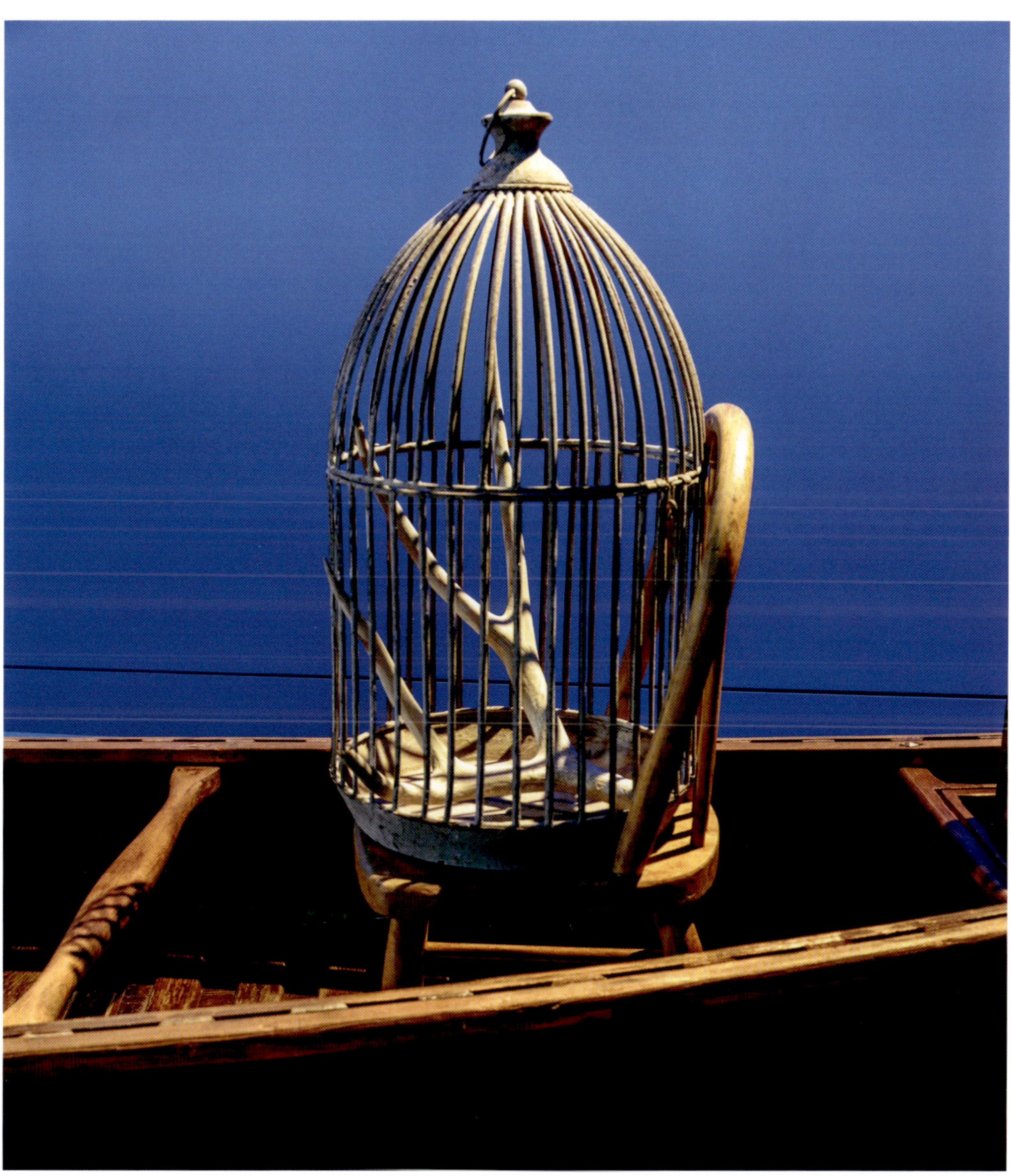
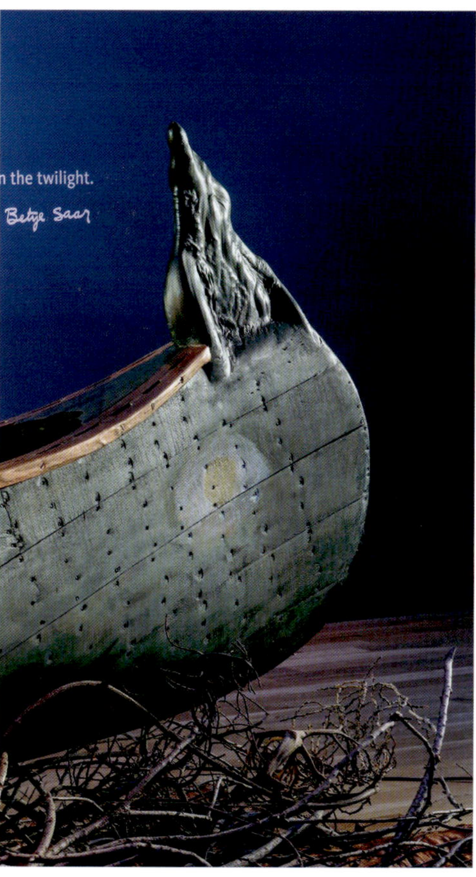
n the twilight.
Betye Saar

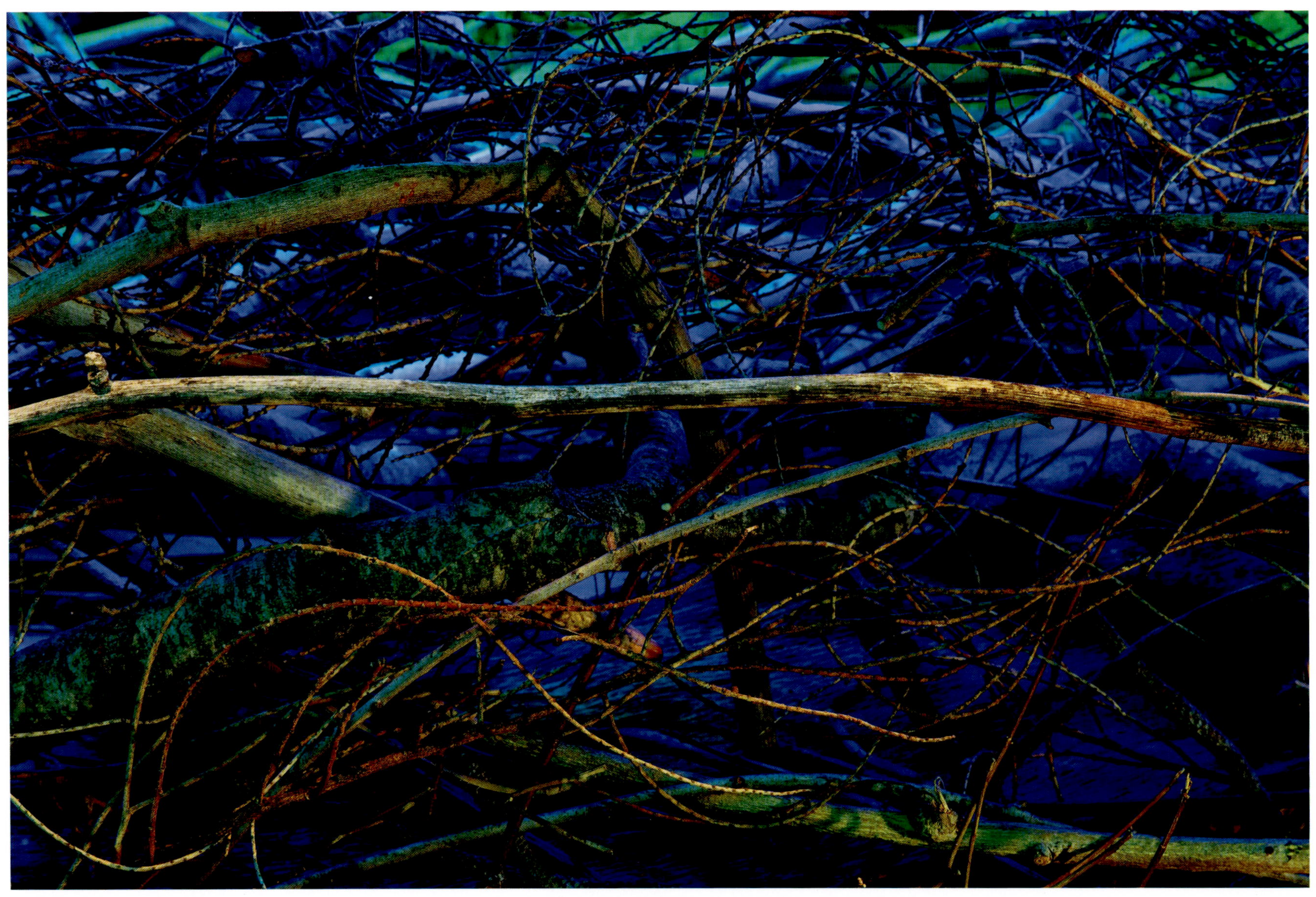

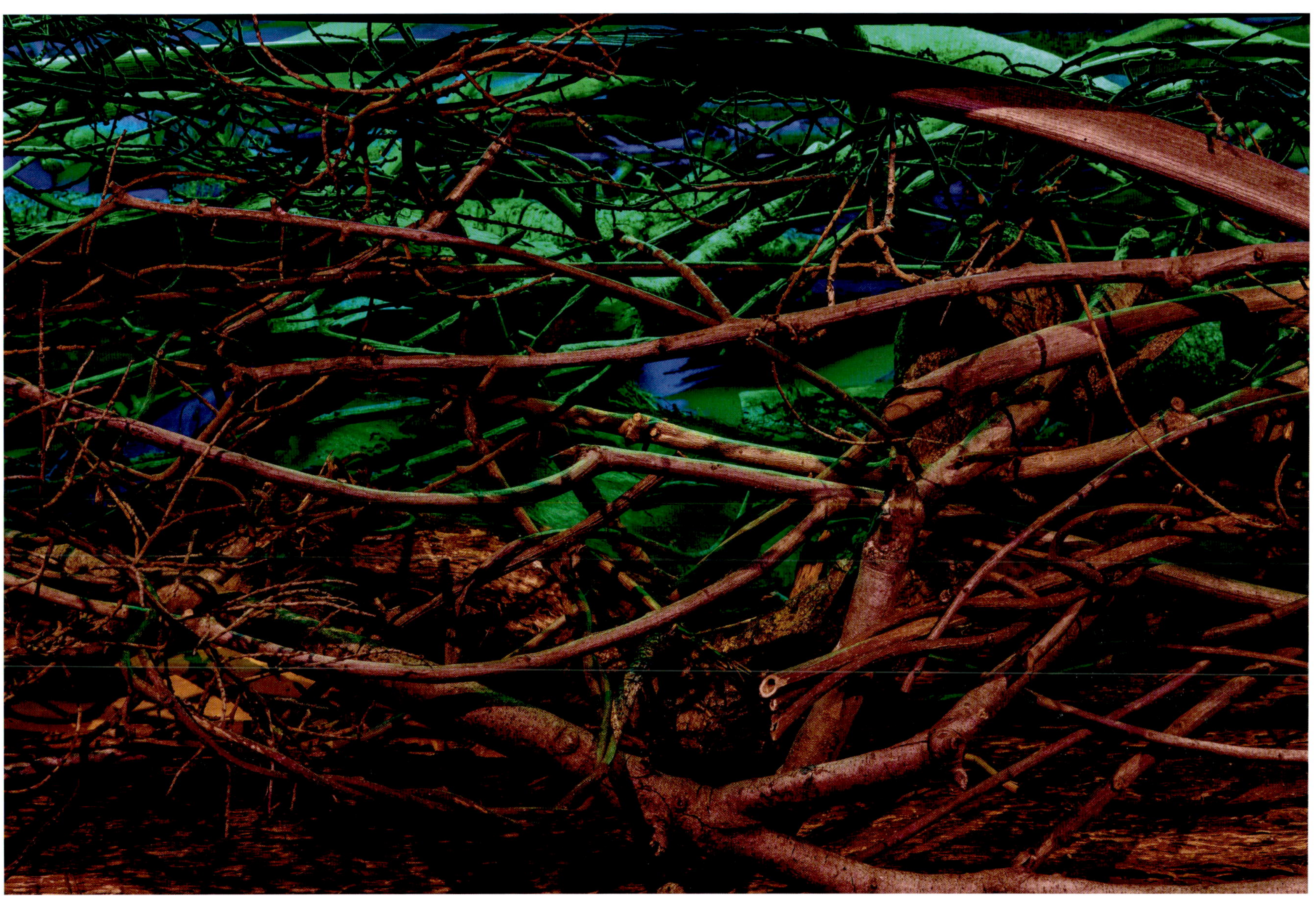

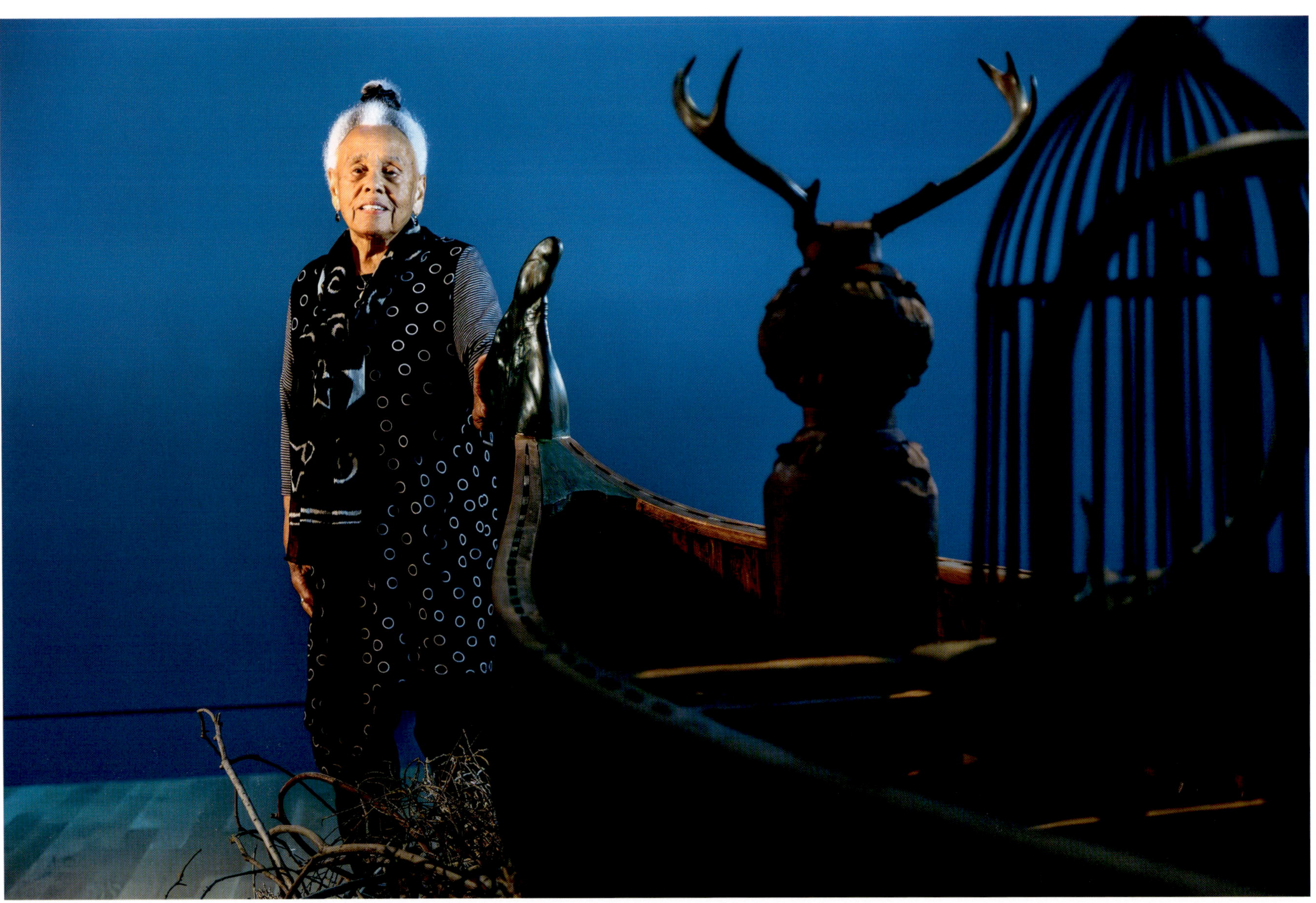

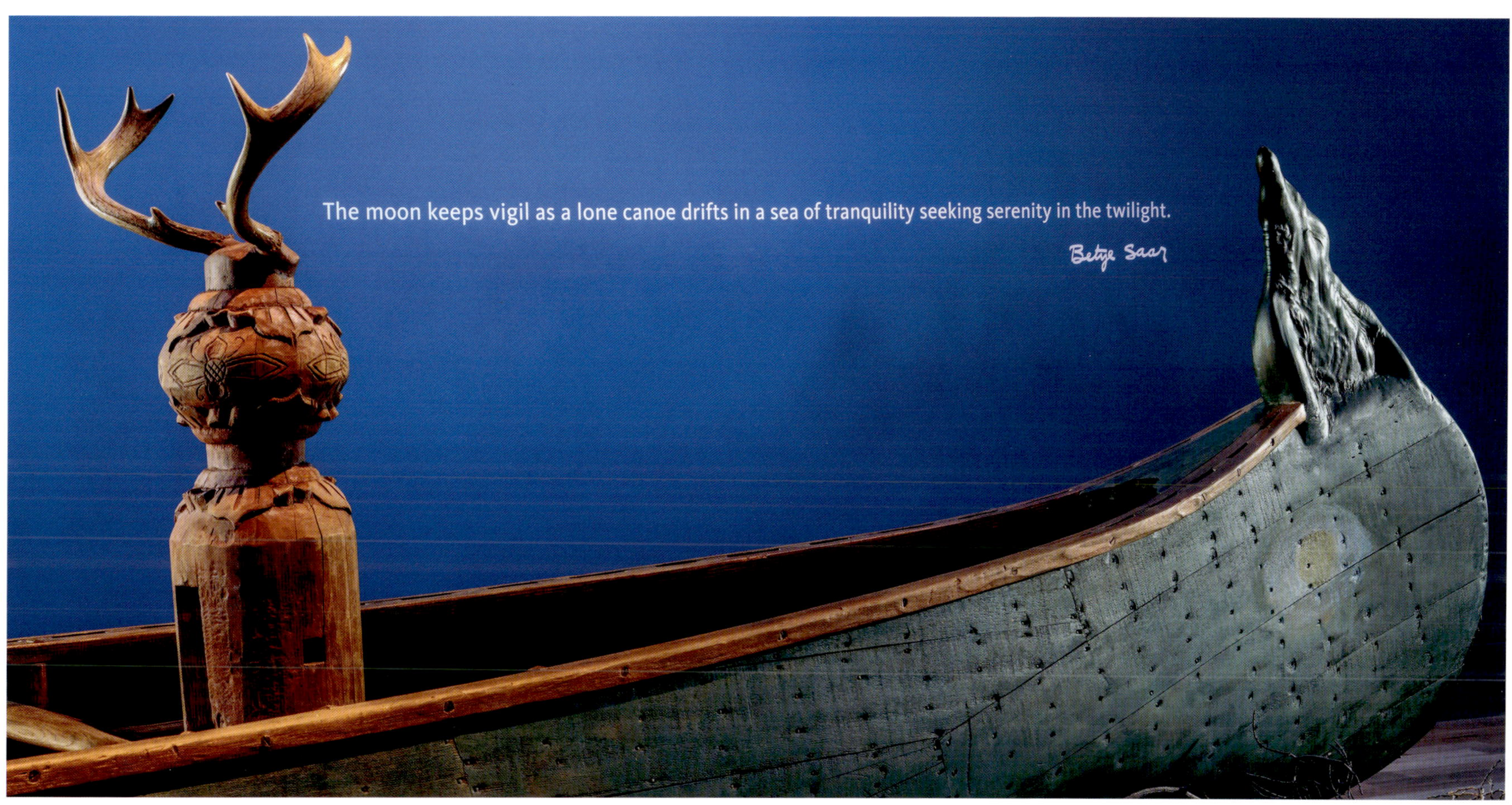

Betye Saar, *Drifting Toward Twilight*, 2023 (installation views). Mixed media installation. The Huntington Library, Art Museum, and Botanical Gardens. Commissioned through Roberts Projects, Los Angeles. This acquisition was made possible by a leadership gift from Mei-Lee Ney. Major support was also provided by the Philip and Muriel Berman Foundation, Terry Perucca and Annette Serrurier, Faye and Robert C. Davidson Jr., and the Virginia Steele Scott Endowment for American Art, 2023.15

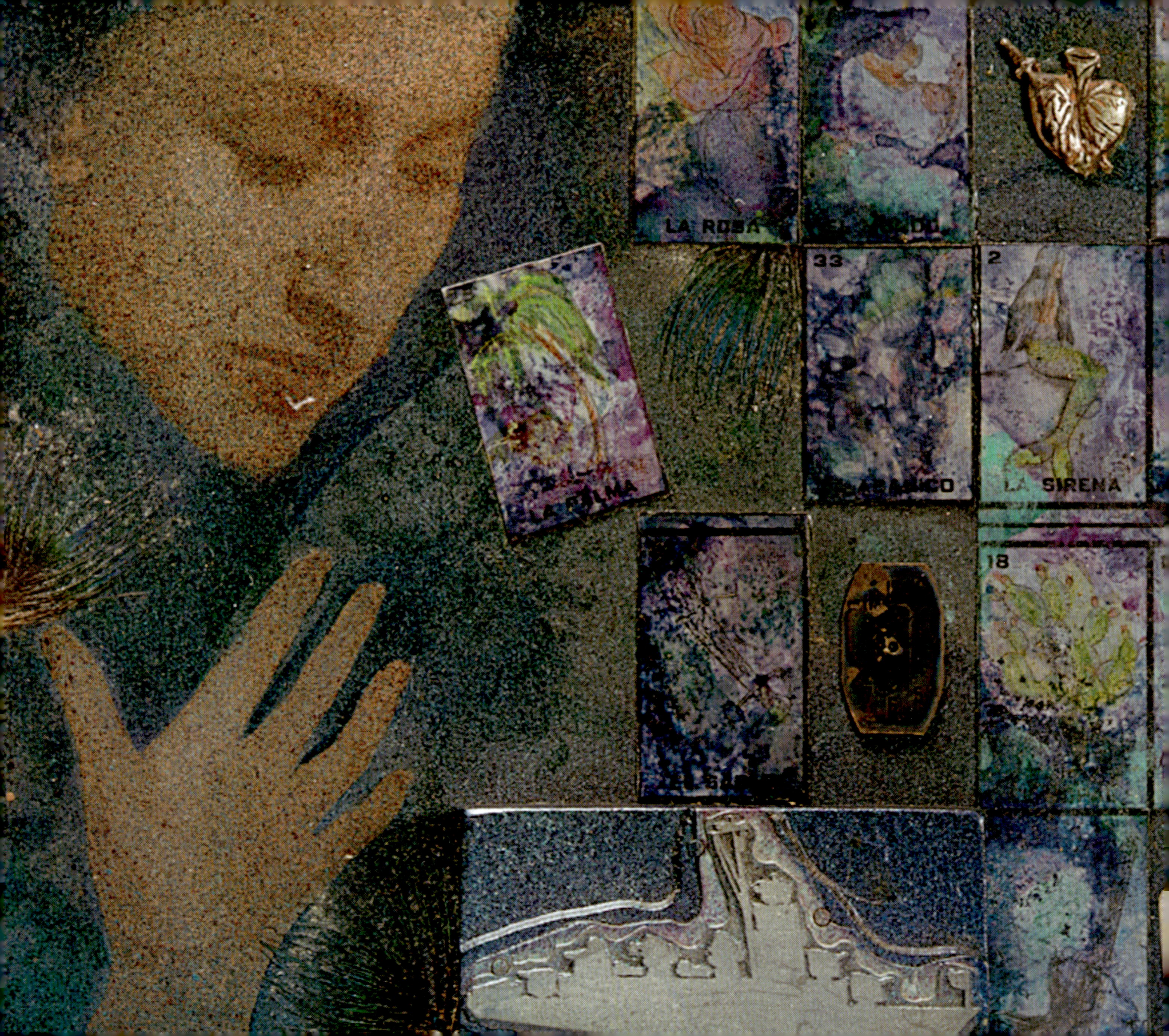
LA ROSA
33
2
LA SIRENA
18

YINSHI LERMAN-TAN

BETYE SAAR'S SEA OF DREAMS

She was the single artificer of the world
In which she sang. And when she sang, the sea,
Whatever self it had, became the self
That was her song, for she was the maker.

—Wallace Stevens, "The Idea of Order at Key West," 1934

The moon keeps vigil as a lone canoe drifts in a
sea of tranquility seeking serenity in the twilight.

—Betye Saar, poem for *Drifting Toward Twilight*, 2023

At an early conceptual meeting at her studio in Los Angeles, Betye Saar described the feeling she wanted her site-specific installation at The Huntington to evoke. She said she imagined visitors walking through the botanical gardens on a hot, dry day, and coming into the art museum. There, they might wind their way through the galleries and happen upon a cool, dark space. The walls would be painted a watery blue from floor to ceiling, and at the center of the room, a monumental wooden canoe would float above the floor, surrounded by cuttings from the gardens and the glow of electric neon from below. In a small notebook I carried with me, I wrote down two thoughts Betye shared that day, describing her vision: "You can't figure out what it is, but it seems right" and "Water is about transition, dry to wet, being born."

It was surreal to stand in Saar's studio—which looks, by the way, like the inside of her mind: rife with birdcages, chairs, trinkets in labeled drawers, memorabilia from her career, and other objects she has collected over a lifetime from flea markets, antique malls, swap meets, estate sales, and friends (p. 58).[1] Saar, a pioneer of assemblage art, uses these found objects as her medium, like paint to a painter. To be in Saar's presence is to feel the gravitas of an artist who, with a six-decade career as part of a foundational generation of Black artists in Los Angeles, has shaped American art and political movements.[2]

At the age of ninety-seven, Saar is still working. In 2023, she completed an immersive installation for The Huntington, titled *Drifting Toward Twilight*. When entering the front door of the American art building, a visitor must first traverse galleries with metalwork

Detail of Betye Saar,
Ship of Dreams (p. 63)

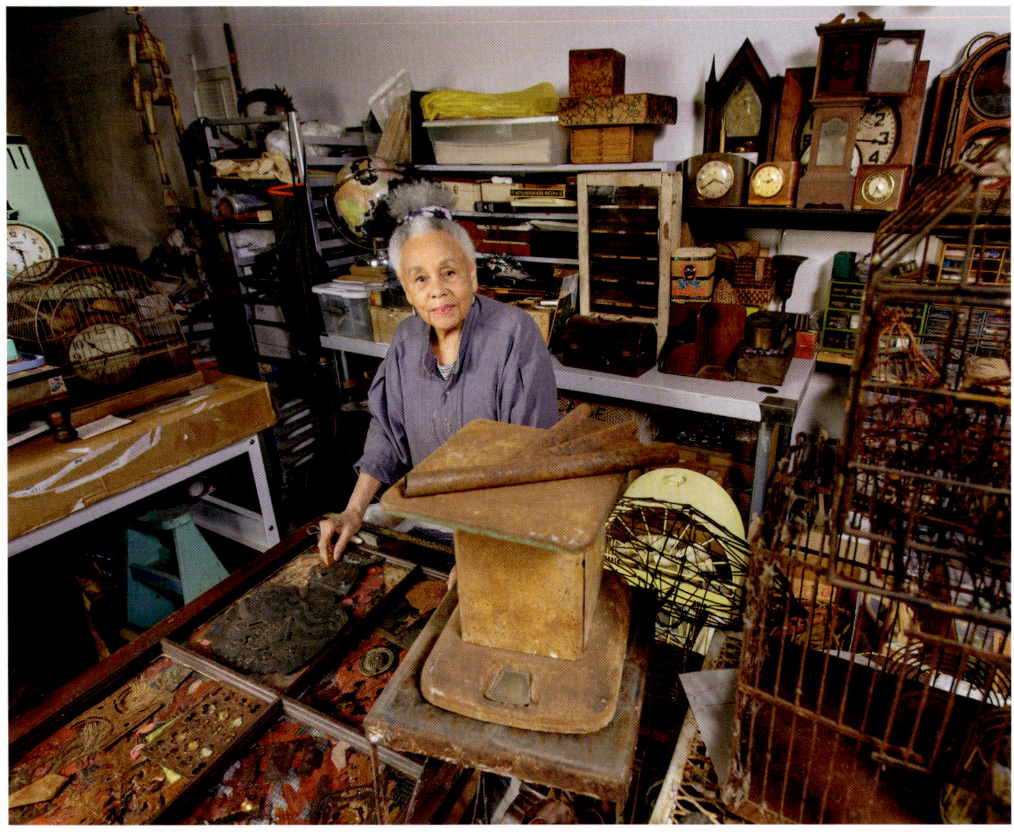

Betye Saar in her studio, 2019. Courtesy of the artist and Roberts Projects, Los Angeles

and painted boxes made by folk artists in early America, paintings by twentieth-century California modernists like Agnes Pelton and Charles White, and past a bright blue Donald Judd before arriving at Saar's room at the back of the building—a space she chose precisely because it felt like a secret hideaway. Stepping into this gallery from the bright light of the regular museum space, one crosses a threshold and the energy changes. It feels like walking into a life-size version of one of Saar's shadow box–like assemblages, each element endowed with a ritual significance, each aspect of the environment carefully calibrated by the artist.

Hovering at the center of the room is a monumental seventeen-foot wooden canoe (see Plates). The vintage canoe was likely built by the Old Town Canoe Company in Maine in the 1940s. Saar bought it from

a seller in Florida, painted it a deep jade green, and marked it on both ends with a large white eye with a yellow center. She affixed cypress knees, part of a cypress tree's root system, to the bow and stern. The unblinking eye and fin at each end give the boat the spirit of a sea creature, like a whale or a serpent. Such eyes have appeared across Saar's work—sometimes the Egyptian "all-seeing eye," and sometimes "the protective eye to ward off the 'evil eye,'" like those that adorn the sides of another canoe work, *The Ritual Journey* (1992) (see p. 70).[3] Inside the canoe at The Huntington, Saar has interpolated what she has described as a "mysterious trio of passengers": three wooden children's chairs facing forward in a line, each holding a metal birdcage containing the fallen antler of a white-tailed deer. Flanking them, at both ends of the canoe, are two intricately carved architectural posts that read like sentries, each with a cylindrical body and rounded head, adorned with a pair of deer antlers (taken from deer that were hunted). The shape of the canoe is evocative: long lines, horizontality, and narrowness all convey a directional floating, drifting, and gliding.

Saar's boat floats and drifts amid elements and cycles of the natural world—the moon, the sea, a bed of tree bark and branches, the glow of light—which she has captured in the gallery, like lightning bugs in a jar or butterflies pinned in a box (as in her 1972 assemblage *Grandma's Garden*) (facing page). The walls of the gallery are painted in an ombré effect starting with a dark, opaque turquoise near the floor and growing subtly lighter toward the ceiling. Inside this blue

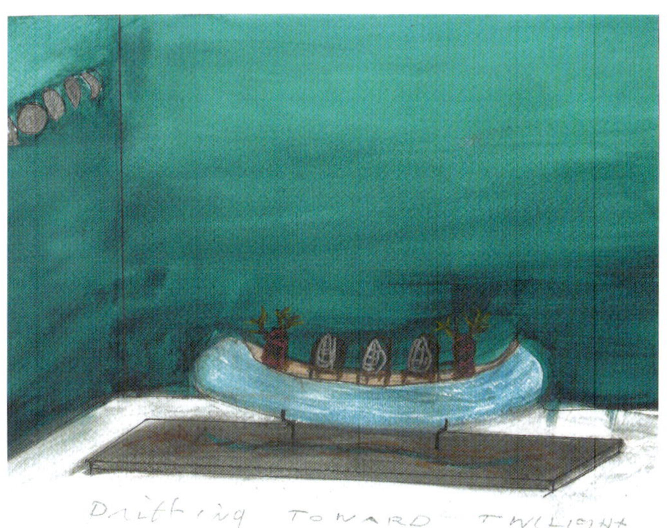

Betye Saar, sketch for *Drifting Toward Twilight*, 2023. Courtesy of the artist and Roberts Projects, Los Angeles

Betye Saar, *Grandma's Garden*, 1972. Mixed media assemblage, 13½ × 11¼ × 1 in. (34.3 × 28.6 × 2.5 cm). Courtesy of the artist and Roberts Projects, Los Angeles

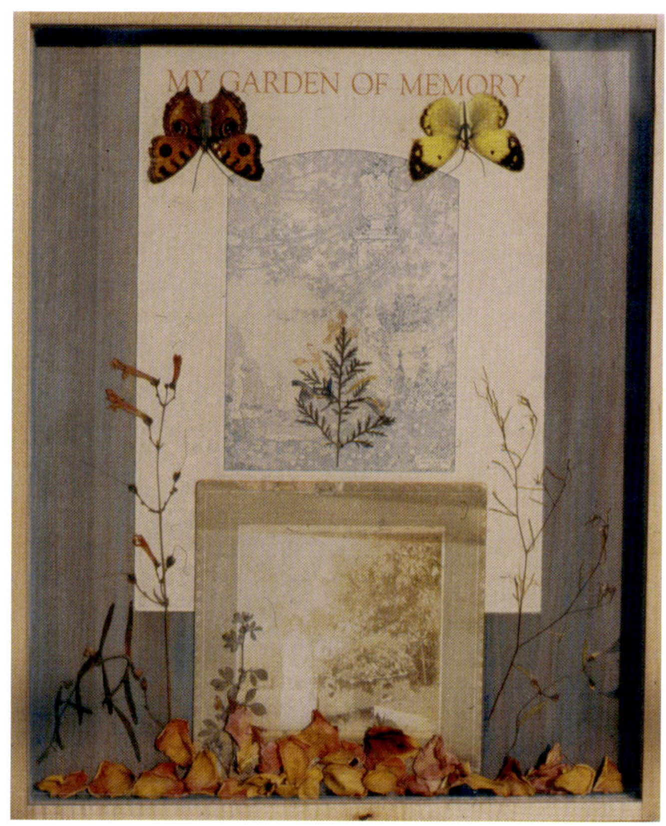

"cocoon," as she has called it (suggesting again butterflies and some kind of transformation), Saar conjures the depth of the sea and the expanse of a night sky, so that one feels as if they have stepped directly into a kind of painterly atmosphere, like that of a Whistler nocturne (p. 60). As in the artwork's titular "twilight," the lighting in the room changes on a cyclical gradient that moves slowly through amber, white, cyan, and dark blue hues, a shifting ambience that evokes dawn, day, and dusk. Along the wall on one end of the gallery, near the ceiling, Saar has painted lunar cycles, the waxing and waning moon, in a metallic silver sheen—a detail that literalizes the passage of cosmic time. Astronomical and cosmic symbols are frequent iconography for the mystical Saar, whose early works, including *Vision of Cremo* (1967) and her iconic 1969

self-portrait *Black Girl's Window* (see p. 26), feature stars and moons, and an even earlier print from 1962 titled *Amid Hallucinatory Moons* (p. 60) shows the artist's career-long obsession with the moon. In the otherwise earth-toned environment, a shock of blue and green neon illuminates the space under the boat with the alien glow of electricity.

A tangle of branches, brambles, and bark reads as waves and sprays out behind the canoe like a wake. The nest of natural materials under the canoe anchors it to the literal ground of The Huntington, where Saar worked with the garden's botanical staff to harvest a selection of plant material for the installation. The twelve species she selected came from across the 130-acre gardens, including African fern pine, bamboo, broad-leaved bottle tree, eucalyptus,

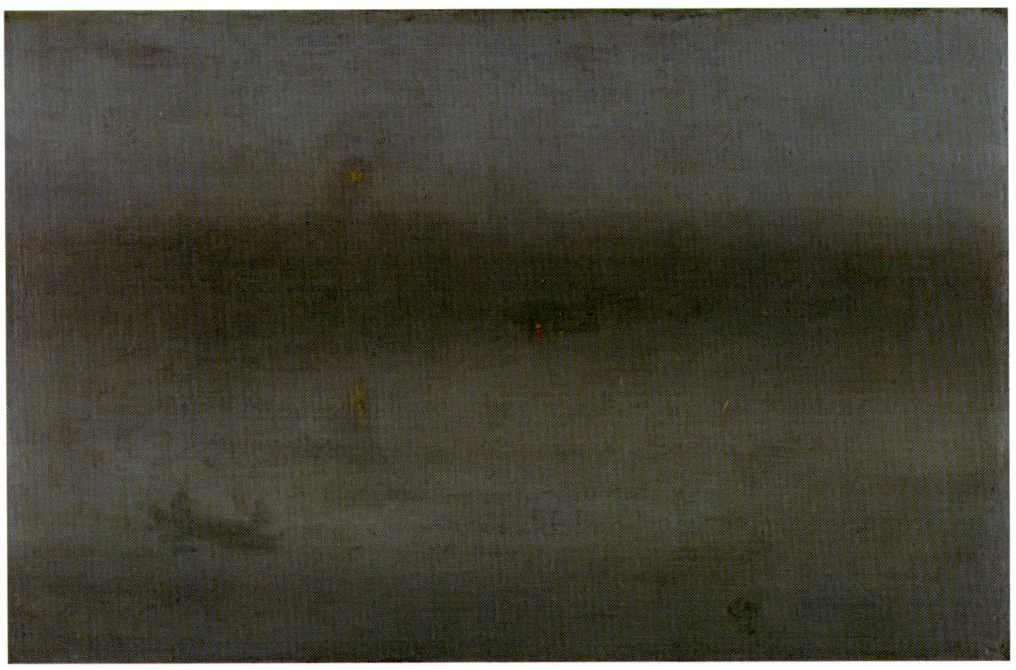

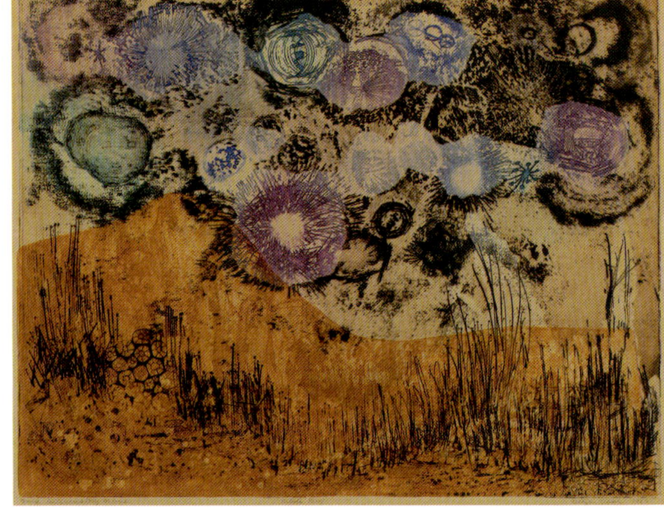

James McNeill Whistler, *Nocturne, Blue and Silver: Battersea Reach*, ca. 1872–78. Oil on canvas, 15½ × 24¾ in. (39.4 × 62.9 cm). Isabella Stewart Gardner Museum, Boston

Betye Saar, *Amid Hallucinatory Moons*, 1962. Color etching from two plates, image: 14⅞ × 19¼ in. (37.7 × 48.9 cm); sheet: 15½ × 19¾ in. (39.37 × 50.17 cm). The Museum of Modern Art, New York, Gift of Julie and Bennett Roberts, Roberts Projects, Los Angeles, 1167.2018. Courtesy of the artist and Roberts Projects, Los Angeles

Montezuma cypress, kiwi, live oak, palm, Phanera, pine, red twig dogwood, and yellow twig dogwood. In line with her broader social practice, Saar explained to Robert Hori, The Huntington's associate director of cultural programs, who collaborated with her on the harvesting, that undergirding her use of plants is her political commitment to social equity and community involvement: giving a place in the galleries to honor the gardeners who meticulously groom and physically labor to cultivate The Huntington's famous grounds. Here in the gallery, the dead plant material takes on new life, and dry branches become neon-illuminated waves. Describing the relationship between water and the gardens, Saar mused, "I suppose at one time The Huntington was covered with water," going on to reflect on deep history: "Most of the world was covered with water."[4]

Sea of Memory

Saar's canoe makes a metaphorical crossing on a sea of memory and time. Saar has used the natural world as a metaphor for memory in early works like *Grandma's Garden*, in which an image of a Victorian garden with statuary (not unlike The Huntington's own formal North Vista gardens) and an old family photograph intermingle with preserved butterflies and dried flower petals and stems, all under the faintly rendered phrase "My Garden of Memory" (see p. 59). We might think of *Drifting Toward Twilight* as a counterpart to *Grandma's Garden* made five decades later, where Saar, now the grandmother herself, creates a world of garden, water, and time. The water in Saar's installation is thick with her own memories, and the otherworldly boat a vessel that is layered with personal meaning. The canoe literally carries the stuff of childhood: children's Windsor-style chairs, all weathered and aged, conjure childhood memories of sitting at school desks. When we were installing the artwork, Saar recalled

BETYE SAAR

aloud that she had artistic impulses from a very young age, around four years old, when she refused to leave the house in socks that did not match her outfit. While working on the canoe in her studio, Saar likened the carved architectural posts (possibly Indonesian balustrades, which echo the shape of a lotus blossom) to the posts from a vintage merry-go-round.[5]

Creating a work of art for The Huntington was an act of remembering childhood for Saar, who grew up in Pasadena and recalls coming to The Huntington in the late 1930s. Born in Los Angeles in 1926, Saar moved to a house at 89 Pepper Street in Pasadena when she was a small child (see p. 85). Jackie Robinson, another hometown hero, and his brother, future Olympian Mack Robinson, lived a few houses away on Pepper Street. She went on to attend Pasadena Junior College (now Pasadena City College), where she designed a float for the Rose Parade, before transferring to UCLA. In a photograph from her archives, she smiles in a college yearbook portrait from 1944 with bows in her hair (see p. 6). Saar also had many formative artistic experiences in Pasadena, where she started a design business in the early 1950s with the enamelist Curtis Tann (see p. 90).[6] It was also after seeing Joseph Cornell's first major exhibition in 1967 at the Pasadena Art Museum (when it was a haven for modernist and avant-garde artists under visionary director Walter Hopps) that she was inspired to make her first assemblages.[7] Saar's archives reveal that she showed early works in Pasadena in 1970, including *Fiesta of the Dead* (1969) (see p. 32), *Vision of Cremo* (1967), and *Mystic Flag* (1965), and taught at the Pasadena Film School, where she made experimental films including *Colored Spade* (1971) and *Eyeball* (1971) (see p. 25).[8]

Saar told me that *Drifting Toward Twilight* is about the journey—but that each person's is their own. Saar's journeys as an artist and a matriarch are present. Saar recalls many of her memories of growing up in Pasadena and her career, as well as her process of creating *Drifting Toward Twilight*, in an oral history interview conducted by her granddaughter and co-curator of the installation, Sóla Saar Agustsson, which is presented in this volume. The interview was also captured on film and developed into a short documentary by director Kyle Provencio Reingold, which plays in the gallery in a small film space adjacent to the artwork, accompanied by an original score by Joel M. Ross's Good Vibes Quintet. As museum visitors encircle the dreamy canoe and its journey under the moonlight, they may hear the sound of the artist's voice float into the room. The conversation between granddaughter-curator and grandmother-artist is a moment of passing down memory across generations: fitting for Saar's practice, which has taken up her relationship to important women family members in early works like *Grandma's Garden* and *Record for Hattie* (1975). Her work has been shown in exhibitions alongside two of her daughters, fellow artists Lezley Saar and Alison Saar, while her third daughter, Tracye Saar-Cavanaugh, manages her studio.

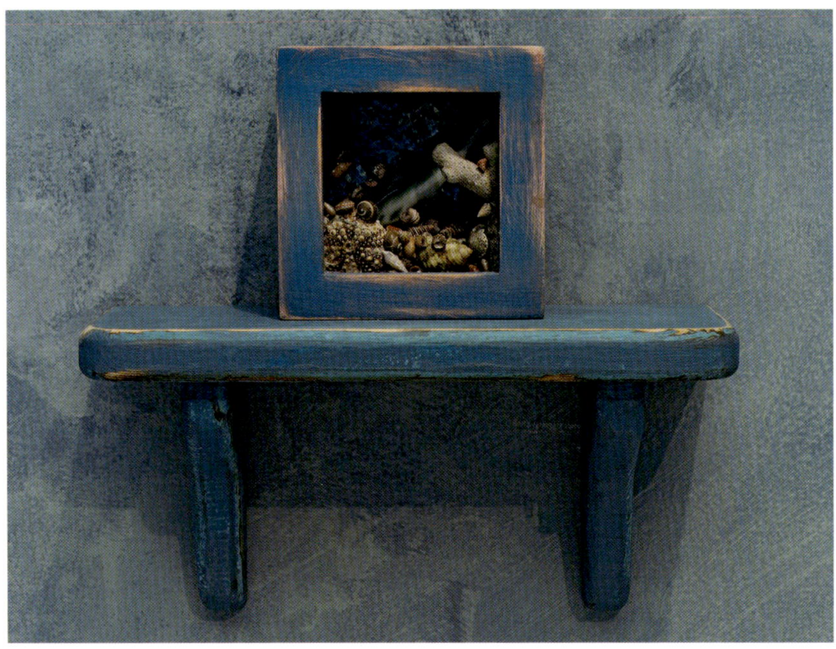

Betye Saar, *Sea*, 2013. Mixed media box on shelf, 9 × 10 × 3¼ in. (22.9 × 25.4 × 8.3 cm). Courtesy of the artist and Roberts Projects, Los Angeles

Ship of Dreams

Saar has long been obsessed with the stuff of ships, seafaring, and water—as well as what scholar Sampada Aranke has described as Saar's "atmospheric reach" in her installations.[9] According to Saar, she was inspired to start using boats when she saw a boat in a parking lot in Connecticut (a telling origin story, since Saar's boat works are always counterintuitively beached in the landlocked spaces of galleries and museums). She began making boat installations as early as 1988, many of which also featured vintage boats that Saar painted and placed at the center of an immersive environment, some also featuring natural materials. One recent monumental installation work, *The Alpha and the Omega (The Beginning and the End)* (2013–16), installed at the Fondazione Prada, Milan, featured the skeleton of a boat with a shock of neon hanging from the ceiling in a room painted in swirling robin's egg blue, surrounded by a number of other smaller-scale assemblage works, including one called *Sea* (above). A reliquary-like assemblage, *Sea* is a tiny wooden box painted blue containing

seashells and coral, sitting on a blue shelf. Despite having a small footprint in the monumental installation, *Sea* economically reveals Saar's almost religious fascination with the ocean, a space that she repeatedly evokes and inhabits in her installations.

Boats and ships appear across Saar's oeuvre. *The Destiny of Latitude and Longitude* (2010) (p. 64) is a wire birdcage—a frequent icon in Saar's work (this one a more stylized mesh cage than the parrot-style cages in *Drifting Toward Twilight*)—containing two model clipper ships setting sail on a sea of hair, surrounded by a wire moon and hands, a crow, and a silver globe.[10] This attention to the sea has often been understood in Saar's work to be a reference to the history of the Middle Passage, especially when made explicit in works like Saar's 2019 canoe installation *Gliding into Midnight*, in which a diagram of a ship that was used to transport enslaved people is reproduced directly underneath the canoe (see pp. 74, 75). However, Saar has stated that with this work for The Huntington, she is not primarily interested in histories of enslavement and diaspora.

The sea in *Drifting Toward Twilight* is more personal, a sea of individual memories and emotions, something akin to her evocation of seafaring in a little-known and early work titled *Ship of Dreams* (1979) (facing page). In it, a woman with her hand on her heart dreams into existence the composition next to her: a grid of Mexican *lotería* cards, a *milagro* (Mexican folk art emblem of a sacred heart), and a ship, all under a wash of aqueous blue and purple pigment that makes the elements appear as if they are floating under the water of her

BETYE SAAR

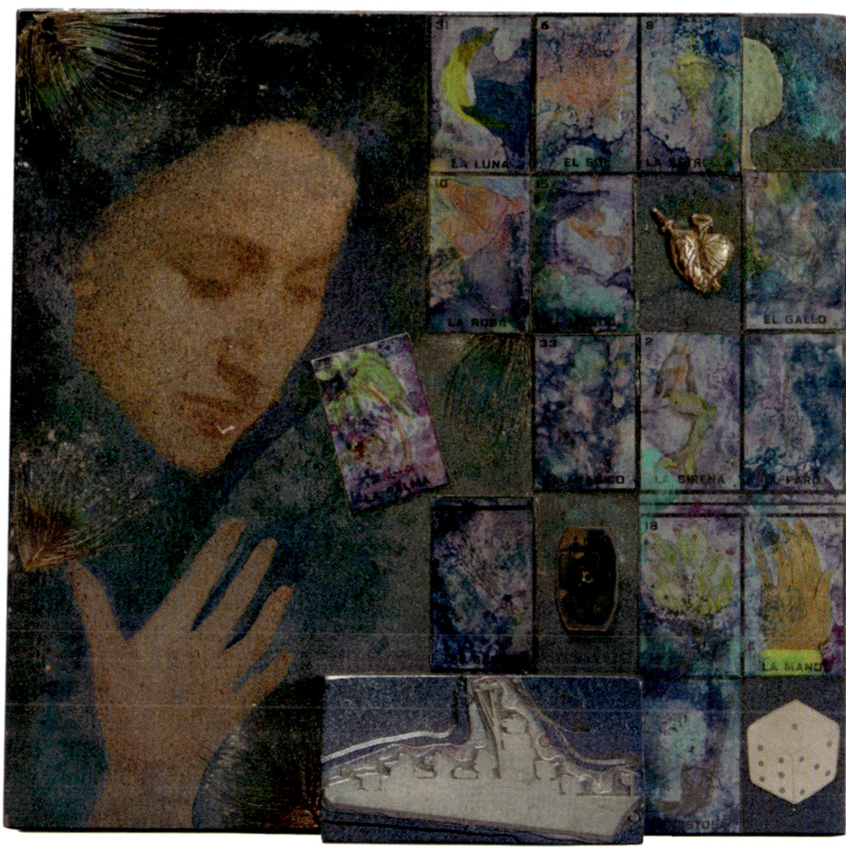

Betye Saar, *Ship of Dreams*, 1979. Mixed media assemblage, 8 × 7¾ × 1¾ in. (20.3 × 19.7 × 4.5 cm). Courtesy of the artist and Roberts Projects, Los Angeles

own consciousness. Although visually evident, Saar articulated her idea of the sea as a metaphor for life in a 2016 interview: "When I think of the sea of my life, I'm not a strong swimmer, and I never had the stroke for mainstream. But the flotsam and jetsam of tides is what I make my art from; I recycle things that I find."[11]

If not a social history, what does Saar want us to see in the sea? She is part of a lineage of artists, including many in The Huntington's collection, who depict the ocean as a metaphorical site of imagination. Take, for instance, as a counterpoint to Saar's immersive boat installation, a watercolor in the collection by the British genius of the seafaring picture, J. M. W. Turner (p. 64). Although the watercolor is humble in comparison to Turner's great oil paintings of harbors and ships, it captures the power of cresting waves at night, which dominate more than half of the picture plane and dwarf the fishermen who pull in a net in the lower left corner of the picture. Water is also the medium of Turner's watercolor ocean, which is rivaled only by the dramatic sky above—with a moon that is not visible like Saar's but is felt in the illumination behind the clouds. Like Turner, Saar evokes the sublime feeling of ocean and sky, positioning us—like Turner's tiny people—within a larger-than-human scale of the natural world that miniaturizes us. Like many British sublime landscapes, Saar's installation has an element of the frightening aspect of nature, something sinister or macabre in the glowing branches and caged antlers (what Ishmael Reed calls, in his essay in this volume, "a high level of spookiness").

     DRIFTING TOWARD TWILIGHT

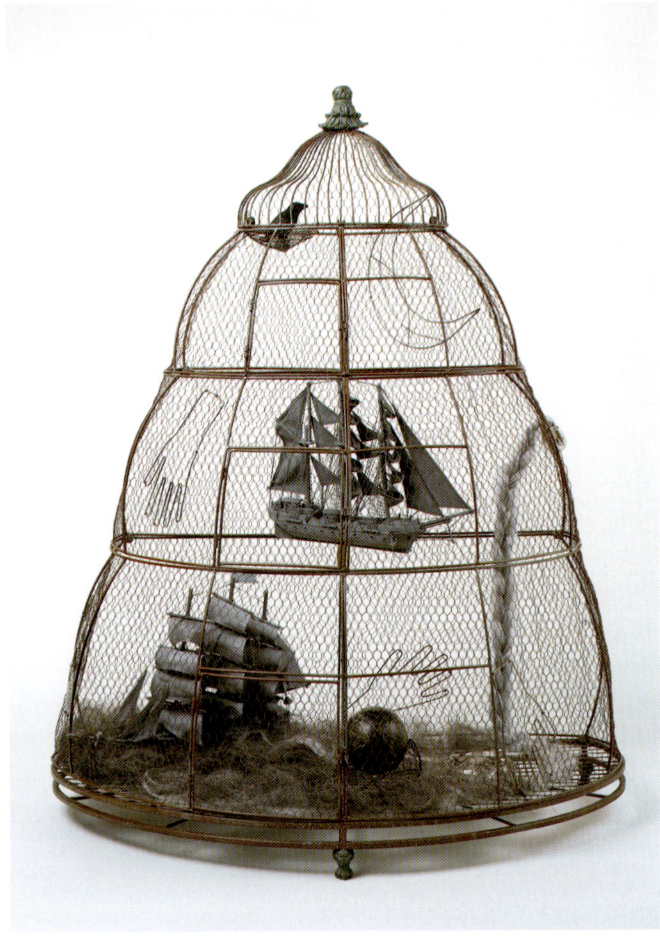

Betye Saar, *The Destiny of Latitude and Longitude*, 2010. Mixed media assemblage, 54 × 43 × 20½ in. (137.2 × 109.2 × 52.1 cm). Baltimore Museum of Art, Baltimore, Maryland, Purchased with exchange funds from the Pearlstone Family Fund and partial gift of The Andy Warhol Foundation for the Visual Arts, Inc., 2020.55. Courtesy of the artist and Roberts Projects, Los Angeles

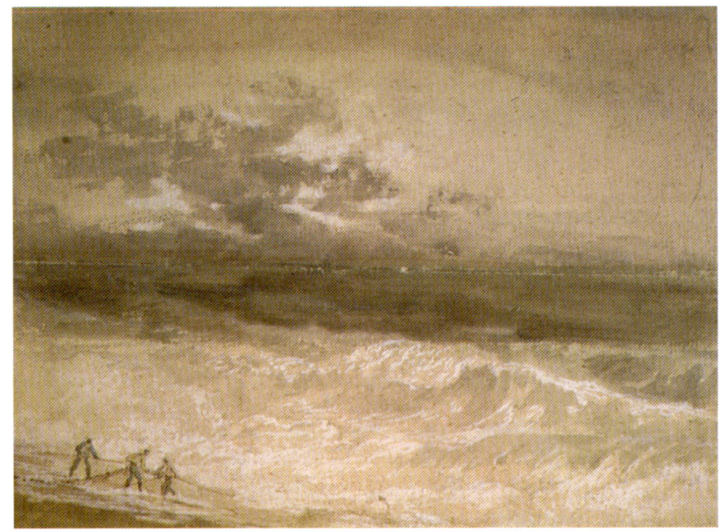

J. M. W. Turner, *Crest of the Wave*, n.d. Watercolor, 8 × 10⅞ in. (20.3 × 27.6 cm). The Huntington Library, Art Museum, and Botanical Gardens, Gilbert Davis Collection, 59.55.1285

Fitz Henry Lane, *Sailing Ships Off the New England Coast*, ca. 1855. Oil on canvas, 30⅛ × 48¼ in. (76.5 × 122.6 cm). The Huntington Library, Art Museum, and Botanical Gardens, Gift of the Virginia Steele Scott Foundation, 83.8.31

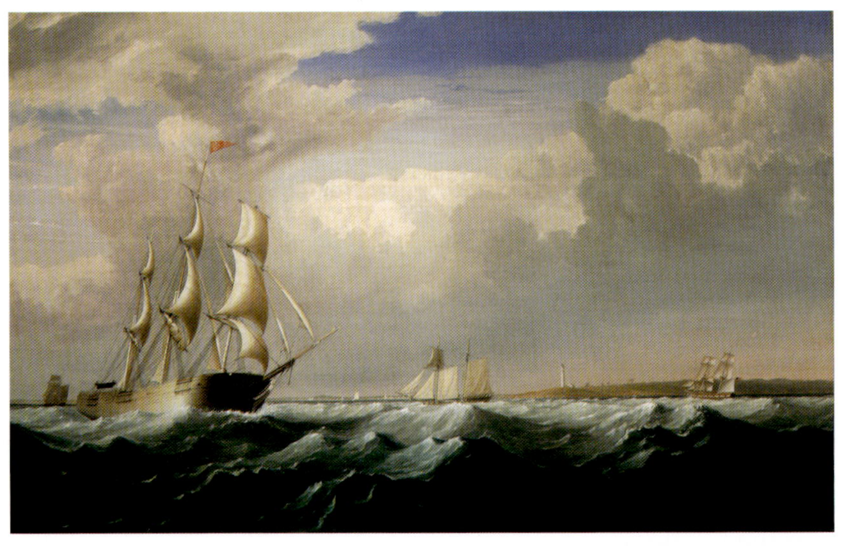

BETYE SAAR

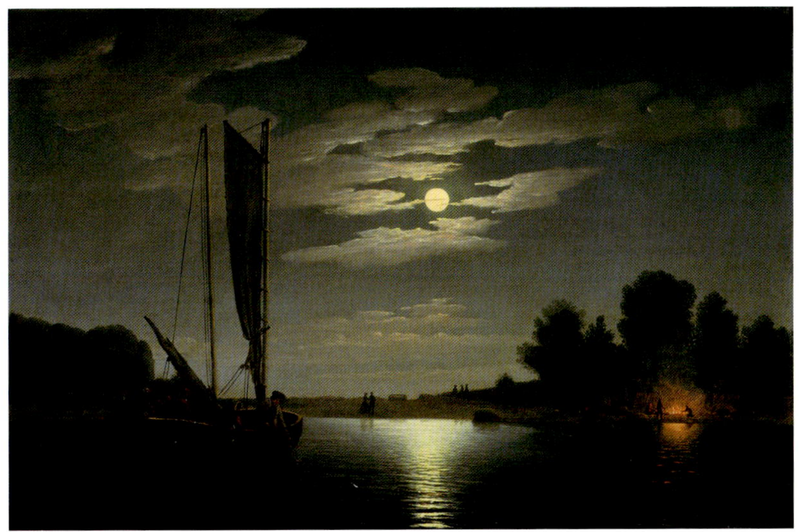

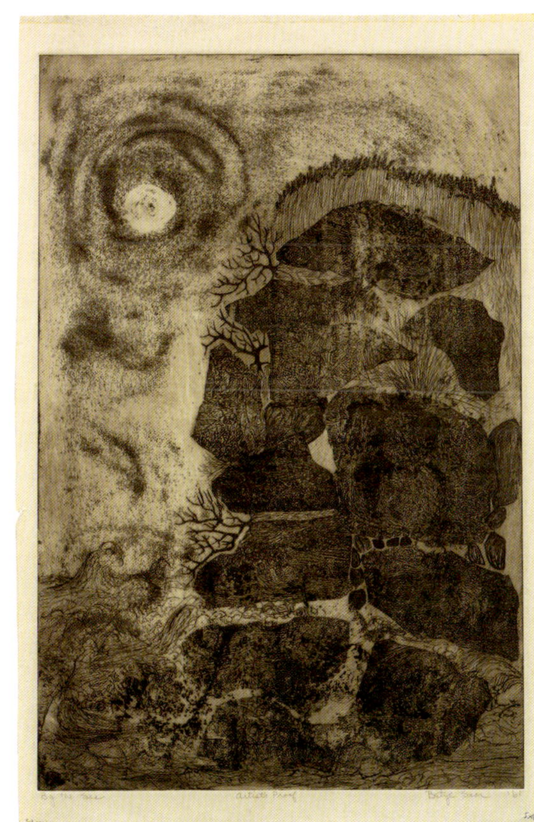

Similarly, just a few galleries and a short walk away from Saar's immersive space and boat is another American ocean picture by the nineteenth-century maritime painter Fitz Henry Lane (facing page). Lane was more literal than Saar or Turner, as he lived near Gloucester Harbor, in Massachusetts, which is visible in this painting of three sailing ships. While nineteenth-century maritime painting might not be an obvious comparison for Saar's contemporary installation art, the deep turquoise wave near the bottom of the canvas (the most mysterious part of Lane's picture) finds its counterpart in Saar's walls, which shift from darkest blue to light, and situate us between ocean and sky. Another Fitz Henry Lane at the Museum of Fine Arts, Boston, *Fishing Party* (1850) (above), feels even more like the nineteenth-century version of *Drifting Toward Twilight*: in it, a boat drifts on the reflection of a silvery moon on the water, and its circular face shines in a gloomy sky that presages the works of American Tonalist Albert Pinkham Ryder. Like Lane and Turner, Saar is an artist who activates our imagination—and emotion—by channeling the scary, beautiful, and affective space of the sea. She asks us to behold the magic of the sea under the moonlight—a motif that appears in her work as early as 1961 (left).

Saar's work in all of its fulsome mysticism cannot be only understood in terms of social identity and history. However, her oceanic interests, combined with her long-standing interest in the Black Atlantic experience and African American identity, connect her to the concept of the black aquatic. Scholar Rinaldo Walcott has described "the black aquatic" in

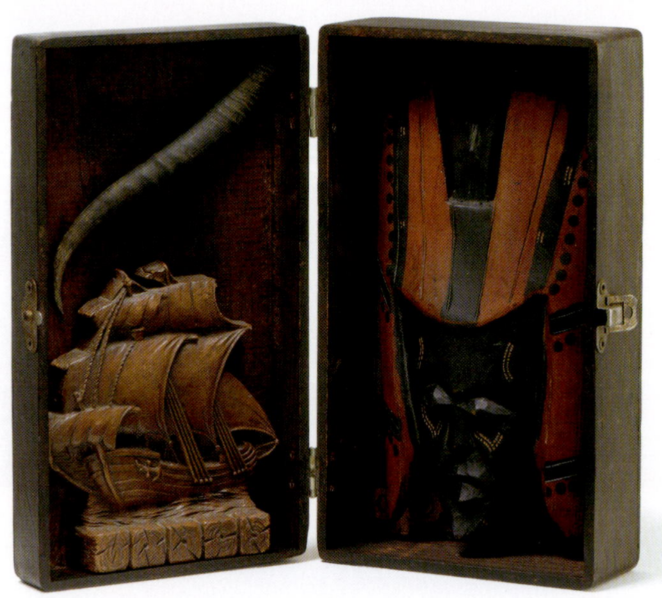

Betye Saar, *Dark Passage*, 2024. Mixed media assemblage, 11 × 13 × 3 in. (27.9 × 33 × 7.6 cm). Courtesy of the artist and Roberts Projects, Los Angeles

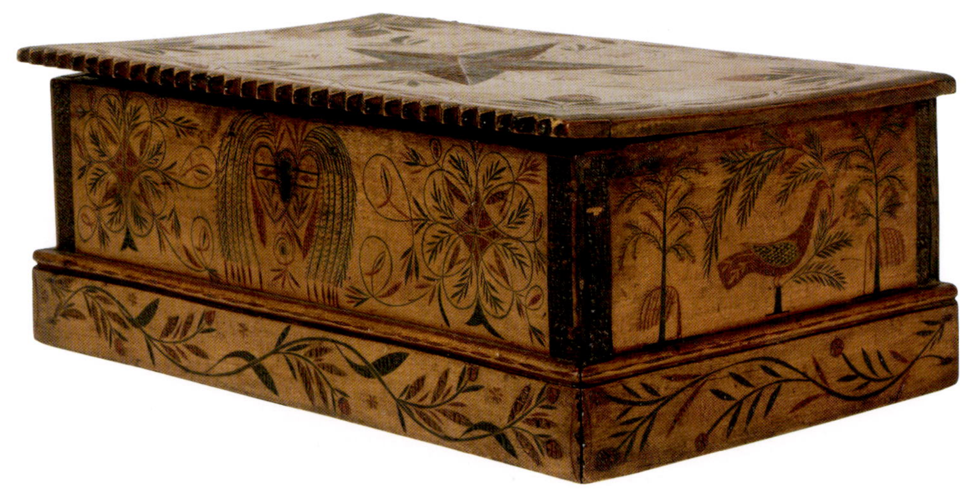

Sailor's trinket box, ca. 1830. Pine with wax inlay, 4 × 11½ × 6½ in. (10.2 × 29.2 × 16.5 cm). Jonathan and Karin Fielding Collection

BETYE SAAR

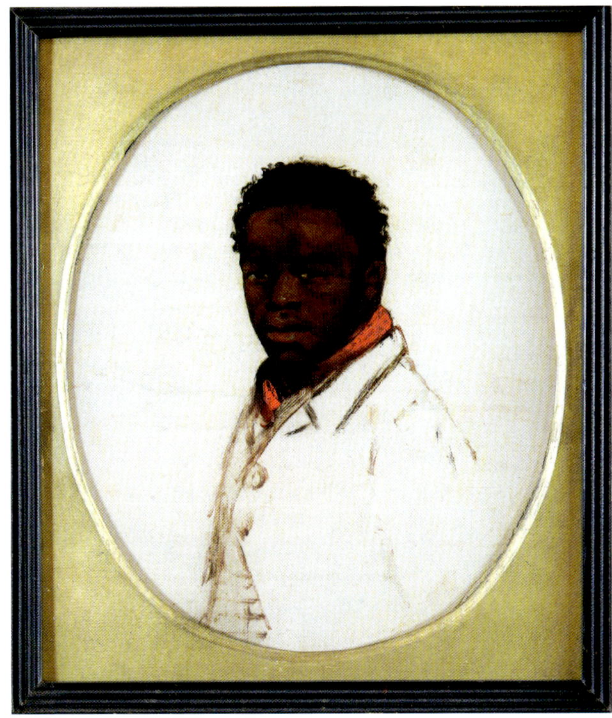

contemporary art as "thinking through Black diasporic life as birthed through a unique and ongoing relationship with bodies of water (sea, oceans, rivers, creeks)[. . .]."[12] Within The Huntington's own collection, we might see traces of this concept in a nineteenth-century portrait of an unknown Black sailor—recognizable as such because coat and kerchief are consistent with sailor costume—whom we can only hypothesize was a free man of color who worked on a British, American, or French ship and the ocean in between (above). In a contemporary moment, *A Portrait of a Young Gentleman* (2021) by Kehinde Wiley is a modern-day version of Thomas Gainsborough's *The Blue Boy* (ca. 1770) and a kind of futurist sailor portrait: it depicts a Black surfer with bleached dreadlocks and Vans sneakers, probably a model from the coastal city of Dakar, where Wiley maintains a studio. Saar's wish that her work be read beyond the context of the history of the Middle Passage shows that it, like these

other examples, creates a space for individuals who are racialized to find a liberatory metaphorical space within the ocean.

Unlike these paintings, however, Saar's boat is not rendered on canvas, but rather is made from the weathered surfaces of the found objects she uses. In this way, Saar's canoe—which she has described as an object of early America—may have more in common with objects in The Huntington's nearby galleries of the Fielding Collection of early American folk art. We might think of her in relation to carved sailor's boxes and whalebone busks, like a trinket box from about 1830 (facing page). Like the canoe, the box evokes a journey. One can imagine Saar picking up a carved wooden box like this at Pasadena's Rose Bowl Flea Market, attracted to the compass-like five-pointed star that decorates its top, which speaks to her cosmological universe of stars and moons. In a 2024 body of work Saar made after *Drifting Toward Twilight*, carved wooden ships set sail inside this type of weathered wooden box. For example, in *Dark Passage* (2024), a ship, African mask, and tentacle-like horn are housed in a box that stands on its edge, like a cabinet of curiosities (facing page). Saar's proximity to the folk objects of The Huntington's collection is appropriate, as she has long been associated with visionary, outsider, and folk artists, like her contemporary and fellow assemblage artist Noah Purifoy.[13] Purifoy's masterpiece, the Outdoor Desert Art Museum in Joshua Tree, California, is home to several monumental assemblage sculptures that resemble boats, namely *Shipwrecked*

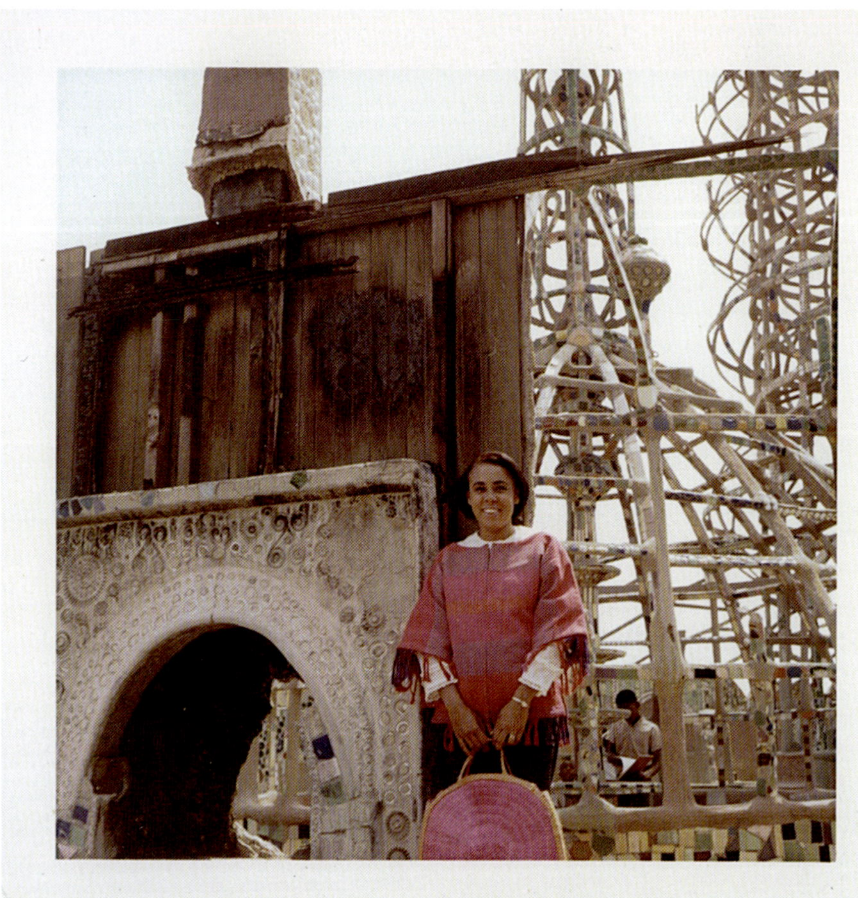

Betye Saar visiting the Watts Towers in Los Angeles, 1965. Courtesy of the artist and Roberts Projects, Los Angeles

(1995), a kind of skeletal pirate ship, or, less explicitly, *White House* (1990–93), which looks something like the junkyard yacht on a desert ocean.

Another ship of dreams, and an iconic work of American folk art, has been a constant influence on Saar since her childhood: the Watts Towers (left). A super-assemblage, the towers comprise seventeen sculptures, the tallest of which stands at almost 100 feet. Part architecture, part mosaic, they were built by self-taught artist Simon Rodia between 1921 and 1954. Saar, whose grandmother lived in Watts, had a formative encounter with the towers as a child, entranced by their magic and materials.[14] While the towers are recognized for their iconic spires, most Angelenos do not know that the interconnected towers form a ship (sailing back to Rodia's native Italy), and its famous spires are in fact masts, two of which are linked by a "sail" of hearts.[15] An undulating wall of concrete surrounding the perimeter of the site, embedded with ten thousand shells, mimics the waves on which the ship sails.[16] Saar credits the Watts Towers with teaching her how to be an artist, in particular the method of reusing found materials. Their humble materials—seashells, antlers, branches, rocks, and the discarded stuff of junkyards and flea markets—buoy their boats with memory. Heart-shaped sails and strange, horned figures are the stuff of dreams. Like Purifoy's boat setting sail in the desert and Rodia's concrete ship masts towering over the city streets, Saar's canoe is a vessel on an impossible journey—to transcend that which confines us.

BETYE SAAR

1. Saar's process of collecting at the Rose Bowl Flea Market in Pasadena is captured in Suzanne Bauman's 1977 film *Spirit Catcher: The Art of Betye Saar*.

2. Kellie Jones, *Now Dig This! Art & Black Los Angeles, 1960–1980* (Munich: DelMonico Books / Prestel in association with the Hammer Museum, Los Angeles, 2011).

3. Ishmael Reed, "Betye Saar, Artist," in *Shrovetide in Old New Orleans* (Garden City, NY: Doubleday, 1978).

4. Jonathan Griffin, "Artist Betye Saar: 'We'll Work Our Magic on It,'" *Financial Times*, November 27, 2023.

5. The stuff of childhood is an interest and even an obsession of Saar's, whose collection of Black dolls was shown in a 2021 exhibition at Roberts Projects. In the catalogue for that exhibition, curator Rachel Federman wrote that Saar can "ascribe a metaphysical significance to childhood things." Betye Saar et al., *Betye Saar: Black Doll Blues* (Los Angeles: Roberts Projects, 2022), 151.

6. Sebastian Grant, "Curtis Tann: Almost Lost to Time," *Art Jewelry Forum*, February 16, 2022, https://artjewelryforum .org/articles/curtis-tann -almost-lost-to-time/.

7. Marci Kwon, "Black Magic," in *Enchantments: Joseph Cornell and American Modernism* (Princeton, NJ: Princeton University Press, 2021), 191; Helen Molesworth, Linda Goode Bryant, and Marci Kwon, "Betye Saar: Working My Mojo," *Recording Artists: Radical Women*, Getty podcast, November 12, 2019, https://www.getty.edu /recordingartists/season-1 /saar/.

8. "Betye Saar Ledgers" (n.d.), Betye Saar Papers, Roberts Projects, Los Angeles.

9. Sampada Aranke, "Betye Saar's Atmospheric Reach," in *Betye Saar: Serious Moonlight*, ed. Stephanie Seidel (New York: DelMonico Books in association with the Institute of Contemporary Art, Miami, 2022), 38.

10. Kavior Moon, "Betye Saar, Roberts Projects," *Artforum* 55, no. 5 (January 2017), https://www.artforum.com /events/betye-saar-3-226951/.

11. Betye Saar, "Influences: Betye Saar," *Frieze*, no. 182 (October 2016), https://www .frieze.com/article/influences -betye-saar.

12. Rinaldo Walcott, "The Black Aquatic," *Liquid Blackness* 5, no. 1 (April 1, 2021): 63–73, https://doi.org/10.1215 /26923874-8932585; Jared Christopher Brian Richardson, "The Black Aquatic: Affect, Occiduus, and Temporality Beyond the Atlantic" (PhD diss., Northwestern University, 2018), https://doi .org/10.21985/n2-0cq9-vp15.

13. Lynne Cooke, *Outliers and American Vanguard Art* (Chicago: University of Chicago Press in association with the National Gallery of Art, Washington, DC, 2018), 89, 90, 362.

14. Saar, "Influences: Betye Saar."

15. Christopher Reynolds, "Watts Towers at 100: Junk Turned into Art Still Casts a Spell," *Los Angeles Times*, December 24, 2021, https:// www.latimes.com/travel /story/2021-12-24/how-the -watts-towers-were-born-and -how-they-got-to-be-100.

16. Deborah Netburn, "One Obsession Begets Another: A Biologist Yearns to Discover the Secrets of Watts Towers' Shells," *Los Angeles Times*, January 24, 2019, https:// www.latimes.com/science /sciencenow/la-sci-sn-watts -towers-shells-20190124 -story.html.

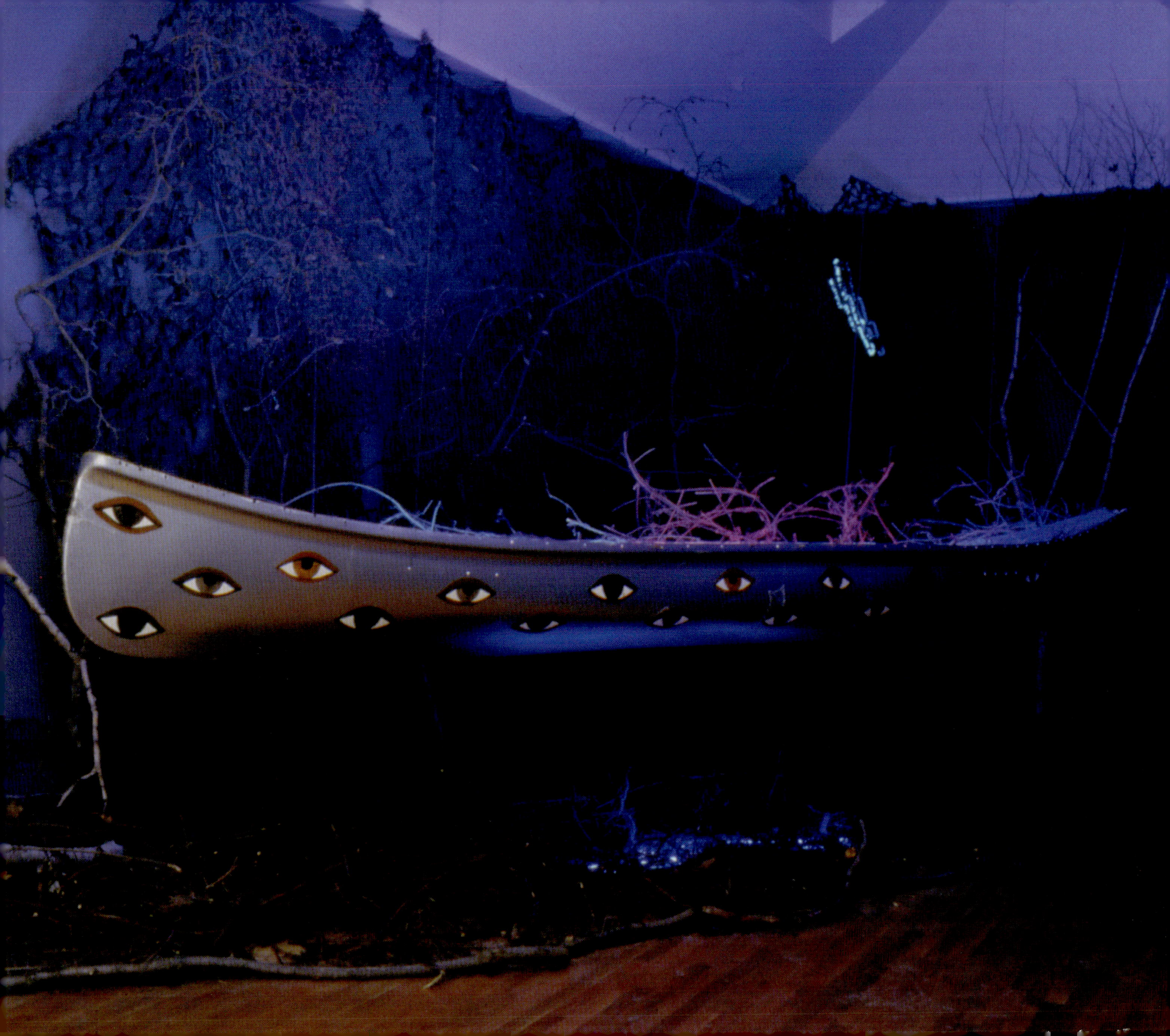

TIFFANY E. BARBER

BETYE SAAR, CHOREOGRAPHER

In 1988, Betye Saar exhibited *Voyages: Dreams and Destinations*, her first mixed media installation to feature a canoe (p. 72). Positioned on the floor, the boat sat atop a swath of reflective material that resembled water. Two rows of painted eyes adorned the sides of the vessel, while candles lined its top edges, their flames dancing and illuminating the space with a soft glow. In the background, two intersecting walls framed the canoe. On one wall, a chair and a string of tube lights hung from a twilight blue sky. The lights outlined the Big Dipper, also known as a drinking gourd, a symbol for freedom in Black Atlantic folklore and the subject of a well-known African American hymn. Painted on the other wall was a dance step pattern flanked by rope and other objects used to farm and till land. Movement as a form of directional guidance under and against structures of containment was omnipresent in the installation, from land to water to sky.

On view in Taichung, Taiwan, from October to December, *Voyages* was part of *Betye Saar: Connections*, an exhibition tour organized by the United States Information Agency that traveled throughout Southeast Asia that year. The tour followed *Betye Saar:*

Resurrection: Site Installations, 1977 to 1987, the first exhibition to focus exclusively on Saar's installations.[1] Parallel to her well-known assemblages that repurpose found materials, including derogatory images of African Americans, Saar began making immersive, site-specific installations as early as 1984 that draw on and depart from her assemblages. These installations almost always feature a canoe.

Sometimes her canoes hover in midair over a schematic engraving of the *Brookes* slaving ship that British abolitionists circulated in printed media in order to support their cause, as seen in *In Troubled Waters* (1993) and *Gliding into Midnight* (2019) (pp. 74, 75).[2] The now iconic schematic of the *Brookes* remains a touchstone for Saar, who retains a large image of it in her studio (see p. 93), as well as for other contemporary African American artists who address the history and memory of slavery in their work. At other times, Saar's canoes rest on the ground, as in *Voyages*. In all cases, the canoe represents a journey of self-discovery and exploration. It is also a symbol of escape and freedom, and a means of transportation that connects people and cultures.

Betye Saar, *The Ritual Journey* (installation view), Joseloff Gallery at University of Hartford, Hartford, Connecticut, 1992. Courtesy of the artist and Roberts Projects, Los Angeles

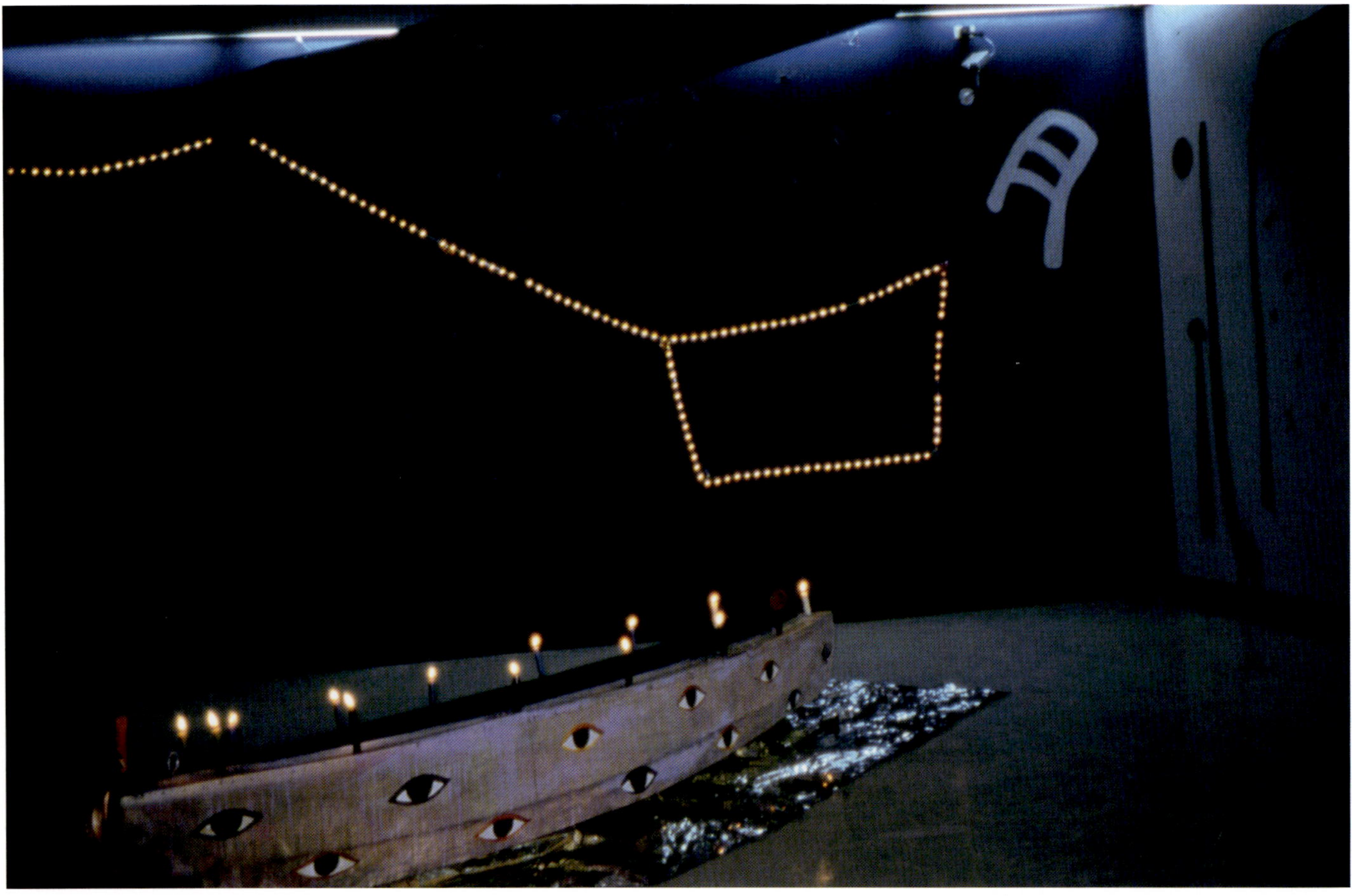

Canoes, for the artist, are portals for movement—from one place to the next, across time and space, between bodies and objects and ancestral planes. In many of Saar's installations, the canoe is depicted as a vessel of memory that carries eyes (that see both inward and outward), birdcages, outstretched hands, and candles (which cast light and shadows). These motifs speak to the complexities of African American history and identity, and the ways that being Black has oscillated between freedom and unfreedom from the time of slavery onward. These conditions have spurred migration patterns as well as oral histories, slavery memorials, African American hymns, and the blues—all of which Saar enfolds into her art.

Installation titles comprising words like *voyage*, *ritual*, *journey*, and *gliding* further communicate the artist's interests in movement. Beginning in the 1970s, her assemblages began to grow in scale, ultimately becoming substantial room-size installations and immersive environments. While these environments are categorically static, elements of movement and ritual—and theater and dance in particular—have always been present. As early as the late 1970s, for example, Saar invited gallery- and museumgoers to add objects to her devotional structures. These accumulated offerings became co-created altar spaces that evolved and changed over the life of the presentation. The first time she did this was at

BETYE SAAR

Betye Saar, Foxtrot pattern in sketchbook, 1983. Courtesy of the artist and Roberts Projects, Los Angeles

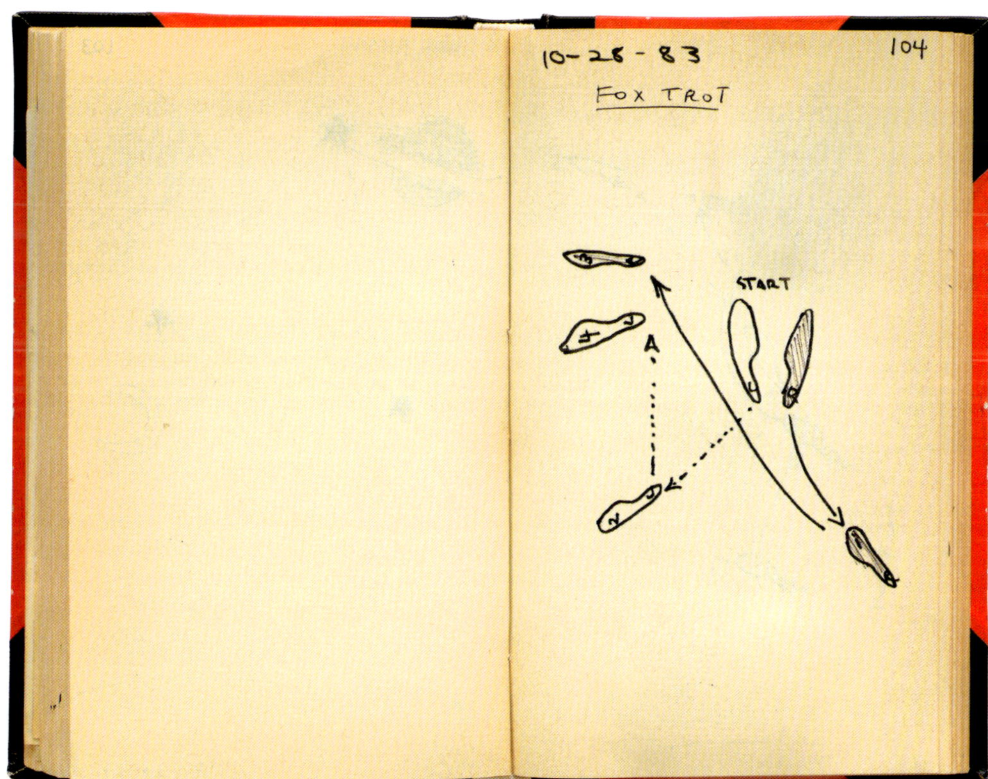

Baum-Silverman Gallery in Los Angeles, where she debuted *Mti Receives* in 1977. Later that year, Saar commissioned a dancer to perform in front of *Mti Receives* at the Studio Museum in Harlem as part of the exhibition *Rituals: Betye Saar*. Thus, by the time Saar exhibited her first canoe installation in 1988, participatory ritual and performance had already become foundational to her practice.

In Los Angeles in the 1960s and 1970s, Saar's artistic community consisted of other Black artists, such as Senga Nengudi, Maren Hassinger, Suzanne Jackson, Noah Purifoy, and David Hammons, who turned to performance as experimental terrain for artmaking. Beginning in the late 1960s, the rise of performance art coincided with various political movements for equality and liberation around the world. Operating outside of a commercial, market-based system granted practitioners of performance art a certain freedom to explore issues surrounding race, gender, sexuality, class, and social unrest. Saar's installations, and the strategies of accumulation that constitute them, underscore how the artist thinks about theater, and by extension dance, as a laboratory for experimenting with relations between self and other. Accumulation and collecting, themselves, are forms of ritual and choreography—processes that the artist turns to repeatedly in her life and career.

Saar's installations are theatrical environments that prompt viewers to move alongside and among objects, patterns, shadows, and other bodies in the space. In this way, her room-size installations resemble a stage with set designs and props, harking back to Saar's early days as a dancer. Saar and her sister Jeffalyn began taking tap dance classes at Lauretta Butler's first-of-its-kind, Black-owned studio in Pasadena in the late 1930s, and the two would make paper dance patterns for practice purposes at home. Known as the Brown Sisters, Betye and Jeffalyn, along with other young dancers from Butler's studio, would perform at the fundraising balls that their great-uncle hosted at the local Nine o' Clock Club, where he was a member. Years later, the artist took elective dance classes at Pasadena City College as supplements to her fine art training.[3] "Most of my interests in life have been divided between art and theater," Saar declares in a recent interview for *Serious Moonlight*, which focused exclusively on Saar's installation artworks. "An installation, for me," she continues, "suggests a theatrical environment. The viewer is a participant in a play or a scene. [. . .] When I create an installation, I want a viewer involved just by walking through. They're not an actor, but how they react to the environment—

that's the action of the play."[4] Reading Saar's installations through the lens of her own dance history and reflections on theater recasts her as more than a maker; she is a choreographer, and museum visitors participate in the movement she directs.

Concurrent with Saar's transition from assemblage to installation art—as well as the rise in performance art—Trisha Brown, Steve Paxton, Bill T. Jones, Ishmael Houston-Jones, and other postmodern dancer-choreographers in the 1960s, 1970s, and 1980s in New York turned to accumulation as an improvised movement strategy.[5] These artists developed a new form of experimental dance-based art called "contact

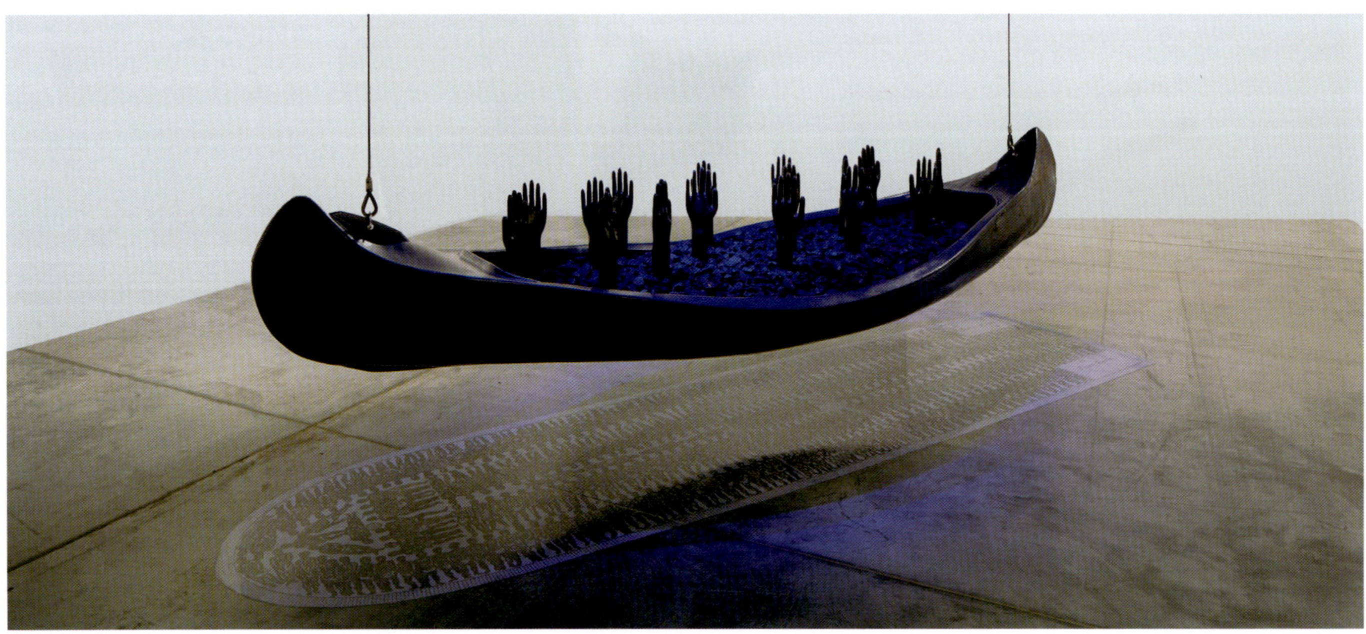

Betye Saar, *Gliding into Midnight*, 2019. Mixed media assemblage tableau, 22 × 138 × 36 in. (55.9 × 350.5 × 91.4 cm). Tia Collection, Santa Fe, New Mexico. Courtesy of the artist and Roberts Projects, Los Angeles

BETYE SAAR

Detail of Thomas Clarkson, *Stowage of the British Slave Ship "Brookes" under the Regulated Slave Trade Act of 1788*, etching. Plymouth Chapter of the Society for Effecting the Abolition of the Slave Trade, ca. 1788

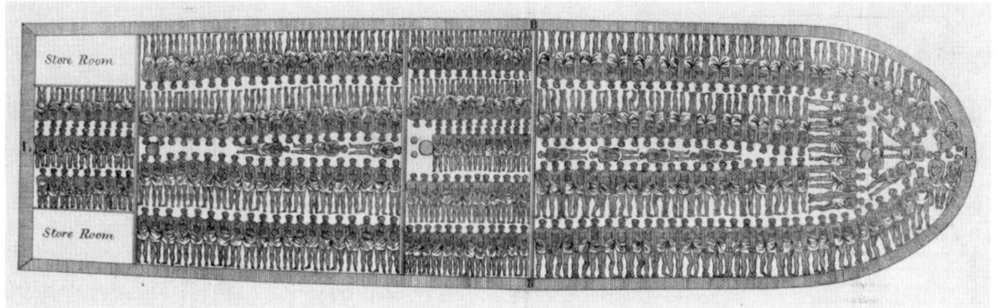

improvisation"—a movement vocabulary that consists of compositional exercises and gestures spurred by the laws of physics that govern motion, such as gravity, momentum, and inertia, with physical, often precipitous *contact* between bodies in space. Contact improvisation can be free form or take the shape of a score—a set of instructions or prompts that encourages structured yet spontaneous movement and exploration, the outcome of which is not predetermined. Contact improvisation scores can be simple or complex and often involve gliding, grazing, colliding, sharing weight, and other points of contact between participants. Against the backdrop of liberation movements and the social and political upheaval of the 1960s and 1970s, accumulation in contact improvisation also became a means of training the body to respond to unexpected stimuli and, in some cases, danger. The dances that Bill T. Jones and his partner Arnie Zane made during the time of AIDS as well as Ishmael Houston-Jones's use of contact improvisation as a training tool for Sandinista soldiers in Nicaragua in the 1980s are key examples of this.[6]

According to dancer and scholar Cynthia J. Novack, early contact improvisation practitioners "viewed the experience of touching and sharing weight with a partner of either sex and any size as a way of constructing a new experience of the self interacting with another person."[7] In addition to animating the spirit of free love and the antiestablishment sentiment that proliferated in the United States at the time, these formal qualities mirrored the "spontaneity in

life, a literal 'going with the flow' of events, just as the dancers followed the flow of their physical contact."[8] Saar's choreographies of accumulation transmute the hope embedded in such democratic fantasies into something else, an "uneasy" kind of dancing, as the artist describes it, that "moves in a creative spiral with the concepts of passage, crossroads, death and rebirth, along with the underlying elements of race and gender."[9] Across her practice, Saar considers how bodies and objects move in space, the basic units of improvised dance, with a twist. Many of her signature motifs—eyes, stars, birdcages—comment on the effects of enslavement and enclosure that circumscribe Black life as well as the everyday limitations that women confront in society and in the art world.

Saar's latest canoe installation embodies the tensions between freedom and constraint that animate improvised choreography. *Drifting Toward Twilight* is a seventeen-foot-long wooden canoe comprising found objects, paint, neon, natural materials, and plant material harvested from the Huntington Botanical Gardens. As one of the artist's most recent museum commissions and part of The Huntington's permanent collection, *Drifting Toward Twilight* reveals much about Saar's decades-long intertwining of installation and embodied movement. Unlike her past canoe installations that incorporated the *Brookes* slaving ship diagram, *Drifting Toward Twilight* is not directly about the Middle Passage, the transatlantic slave trade, or even the African diaspora. The objects and their arrangement, however, express the same tensions between movement

DRIFTING TOWARD TWILIGHT

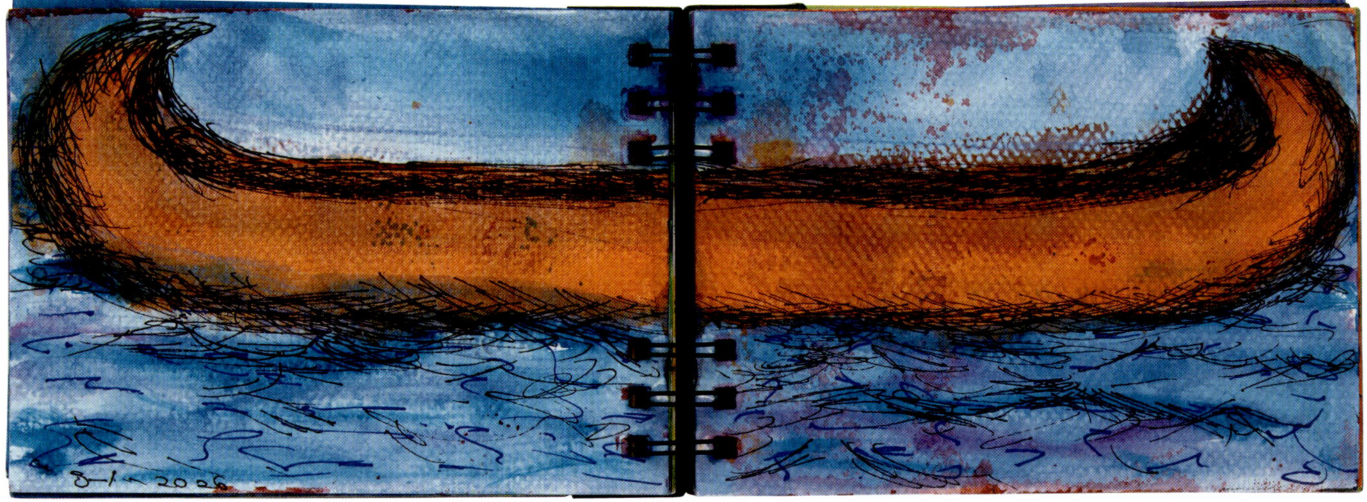

and restriction that are present in Saar's older canoe works. Birdcages, key elements of the installation, are object metaphors for captivity and confinement. As hollow prisms composed of bars, their architecture echoes the structures and conditions of containment that stem from slavery's legacies, reminding viewers of the limits under and against which certain bodies are permitted to move or access freedom. In some of her works, the birdcage is transformed into a vehicle for escape and transformation, signifying the possibility of breaking free from social and ontological constraints. In other works, Saar combines the birdcage with kindred objects and materials such as feathers to create new associations, as in *The Weight of Color* (2007). The birdcage also represents a form of protection, shelter, and care.

Twilight likewise recurs as a material and conceptual motif in Saar's practice vis-à-vis paint and metaphor, conveying multiple meanings each time it

surfaces. The dark blue paint that covers the accent wall of the 1988 canoe installation reappears in *Mystic Sky with Self-Portrait* (1992) (p. 78) and at the entrance of *Betye Saar: Resurrection: Site Installations, 1977 to 1987*. Sometimes Saar's signature blue quite literally marks the expanse of sky and ocean, as in the small-scale assemblage work *Sentimental Souvenir #32* from 1987 (p. 79). It marks time—the twilight hours of the day that the artist finds most enchanting as well as the twilight years of one's life. In her work, twilight is often associated with a longing for a past that is both distant and present. It represents a liminal space between day and night, light and darkness, natural and supernatural, and consciousness and unconsciousness—a state of suspension. It is a time of transition, a moment of uncertainty when anything can happen. It is a space where memories and dreams intersect; where the past, present, and future come together in unexpected ways. It is entrancing.

BETYE SAAR

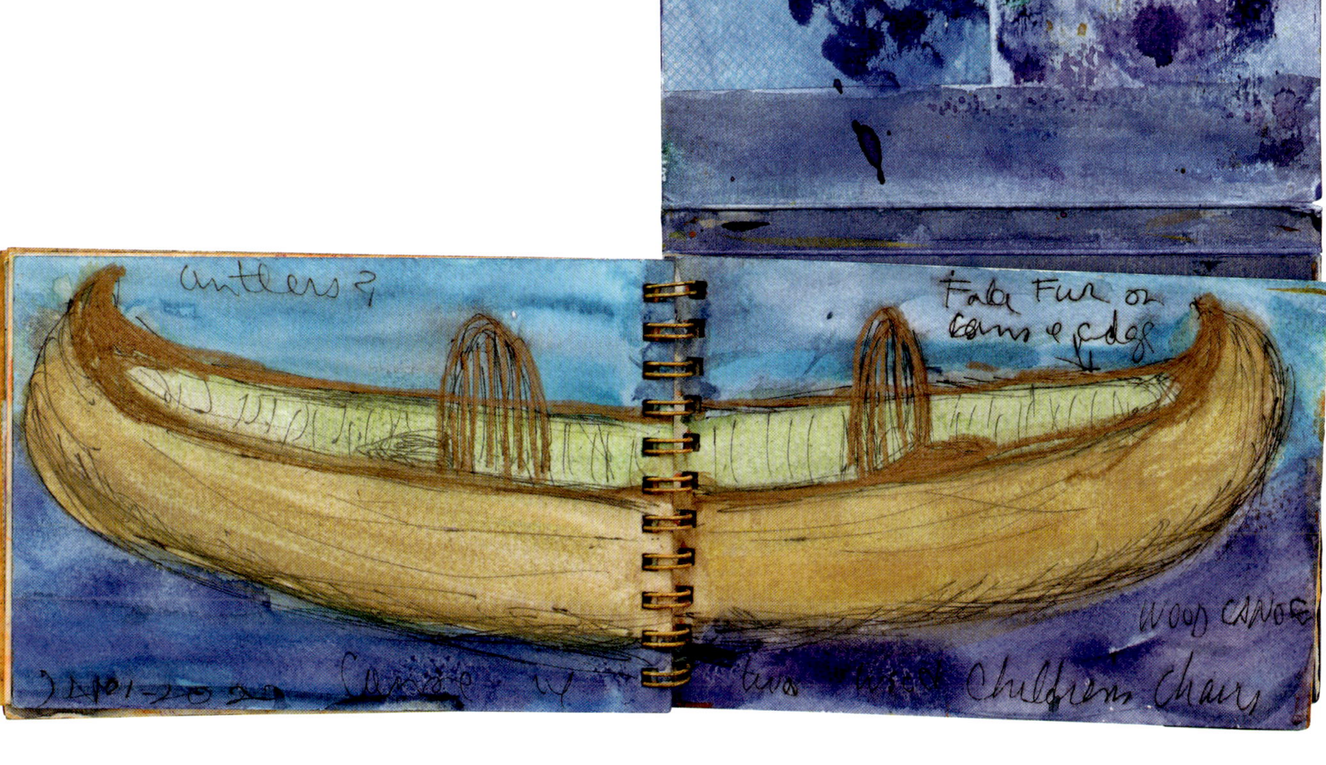

Saar's latest canoe commission and twilight's many permutations across her practice further underscore the presence of dance, movement, and performance in her art. The gallery light itself in *Drifting Toward Twilight* shifts from light to dark in a cyclical gradient, an effect that animates the objects within the canoe and adds a sense of movement to the boat. During site visits and on days she worked in her studio, Saar asked the gardeners at The Huntington to harvest plants from the grounds that might appeal to her sensibilities, a variation on her method in past installations where she invited viewers to leave offerings or to follow a pattern or schematic she set out. The repetition of canoes, birdcages, and twilight as material and conceptual references additionally modulates the social, cultural, and historical conditions that affect how, where, and why people *move*. The wider significance of twilight in African diasporic history and folklore becomes more apparent here.

In the Black Atlantic tradition, the time between day and night is often referred to as the "witching hour," a time when spirits and ghosts are more active.

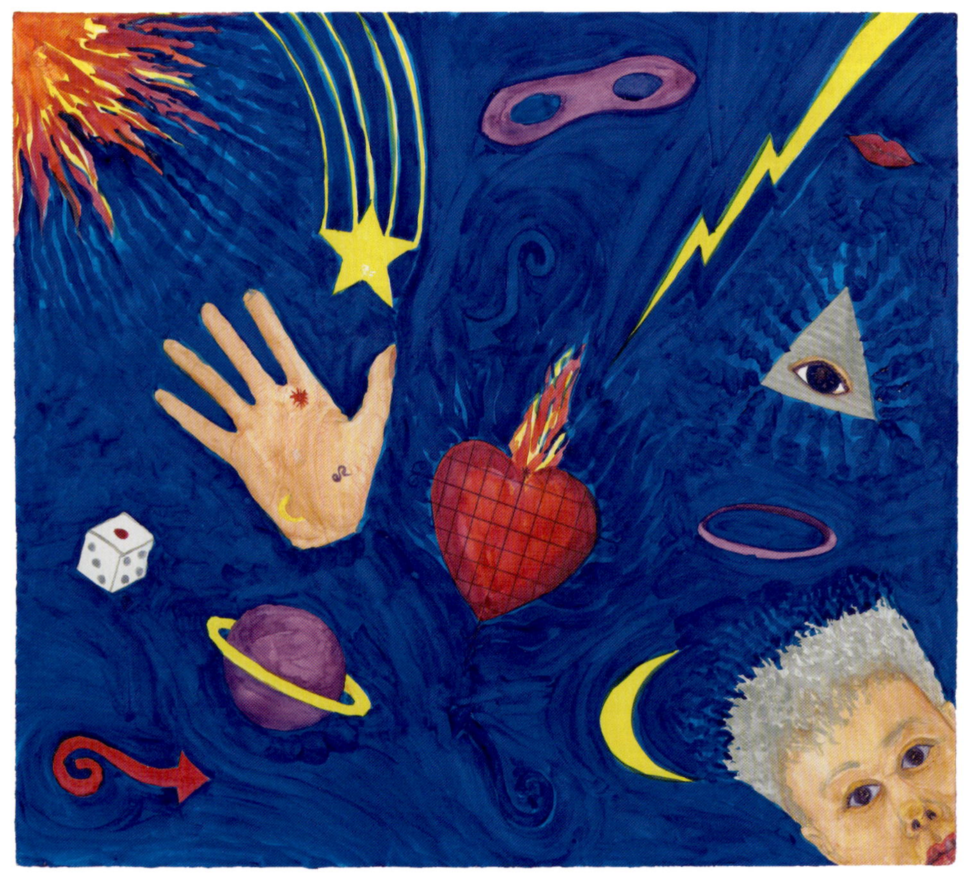

Betye Saar, *Mystic Sky with Self-Portrait*, 1992. Watercolor on paper, 21⅞ × 25 in. (63.5 × 55.6 cm). Courtesy of the artist and Roberts Projects, Los Angeles

Dance is critical to activating such mediums. Twilight and dance go hand in hand, and the juxtaposition of twilight sky and the dance step patterns that recur in Saar's room-size installations—a "static thing," according to Saar, "that implies action"—reinforce this.[10] Drifting—dancing—toward twilight in the artist's installations, therefore, constitutes a suspended space of possibility and transformation. Her canoe compositions of the past thirty-five years consequently demonstrate that choreographing new subject-object relations at every level, from water to ground to sky, is not only possible but also necessary for paving alternative ways forward.

1. *Betye Saar: Resurrection: Site Installations, 1977 to 1987* was on view February 6–March 6, 1988, at the Visual Arts Center at California State University, Fullerton.

2. The wooden ironing board in Saar's *I'll Bend But I Will Not Break* (1998), which stands in front of a pressed white fabric emblazoned with the initials of the Ku Klux Klan, features a diagram of the *Brookes* seared into its surface. Although the ironing board and the canoe serve very different functions in the world, their shapes rhyme.

3. Quoted in email from Julie Roberts to Yinshi Lerman-Tan, October 20, 2023.

4. Leah Ollman, "Activism of the Interior: A Conversation with Betye Saar," in *Betye Saar: Serious Moonlight*, ed. Stephanie Seidel (New York: DelMonico Books in association with the Institute of Contemporary Art, Miami, 2022), 12.

5. Perhaps the most famous example of this is Trisha Brown's *Accumulation with Talking Plus Watermotor*, a solo she premiered in 1978 that built on two previous solos, *Accumulation* of 1971 and *Watermotor*, also of 1978, in which she simultaneously recited stories and performed improvised phrases that were neither mimetic nor didactic. Memories and movement

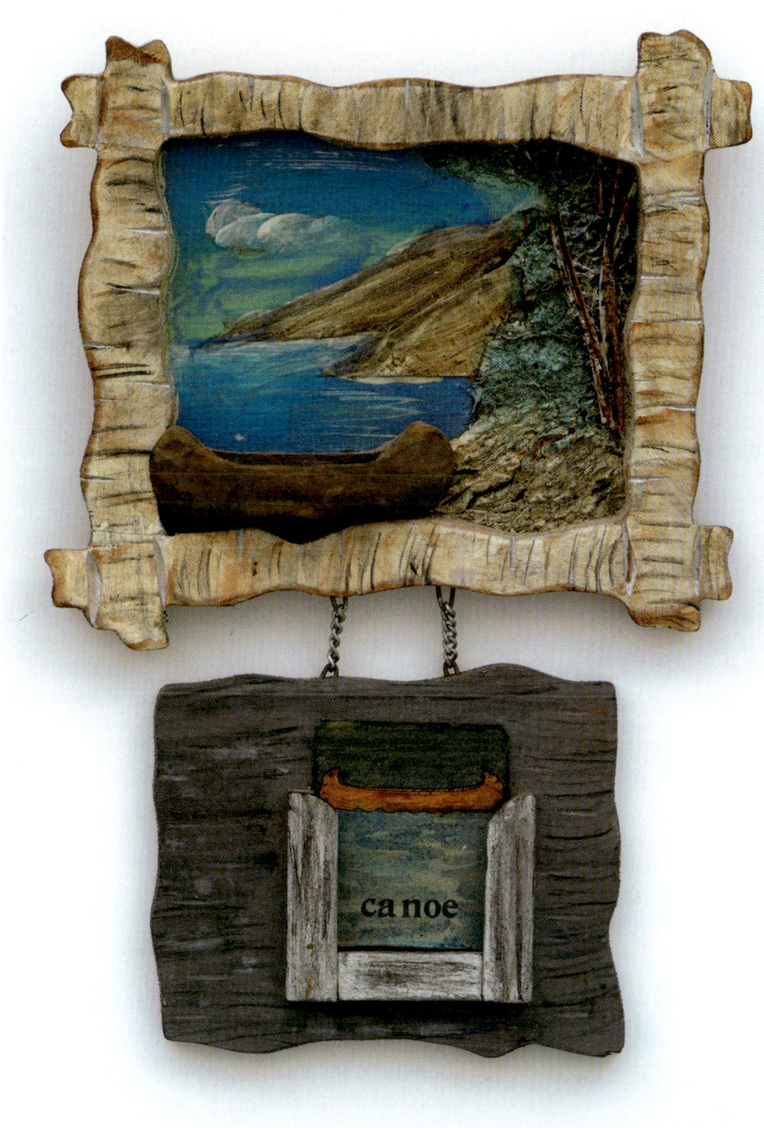

Betye Saar, *Sentimental Souvenir #32*, 1987. Mixed media assemblage, 7¾ × 4¾ × ¾ in. (19.7 × 12.1 × 1.9 cm). Courtesy of the artist and Roberts Projects, Los Angeles

accumulate as the piece unfolds. The spoken score and the movement score do not mirror each other; the indeterminacy of when and how recited phrases will (or will not) sync up to movement phrases, the pauses and moments of suspension, and the collisions between word and dancing image define the piece's contours. During the span of years that Brown explored accumulation to make dances, Saar crystallized her own ideas about accumulation as an art practice and strategy. Upon encountering art historian Arnold Rubin's May 1975 *Artforum* article "Accumulation: Power and Display in African Sculpture," she began to understand her assemblages as African-derived expressions of power and sacred elements that could spur both positive and negative effects and feelings. For these reflections and further context regarding Saar and accumulation, see Betye Saar, "Influences: Betye Saar," *Frieze* (September 27, 2016), https://www.frieze .com/article/influences-betye -saar; and Hilton Als, "Betye Saar Reassembles the Lives of Black Women," in this volume.

6. For more of this history, see Tiffany E. Barber, "Us, *THEM*, and High-Risk Dancing," *InVisible Culture: An Electronic Journal for Visual Culture* 29 (December 2018), https://ivc .lib.rochester.edu/us-them -and-high-risk-dancing/.

7. Cynthia J. Novack, *Sharing the Dance: Contact Improvisation and American Culture* (Madison: University of Wisconsin Press, 1990), 11.

8. Novack, *Sharing the Dance*, 11. Dance studies scholar Susan Leigh Foster likewise situates the lunch counter sit-ins of 1960, the ACT UP die-ins of the late 1980s, and the Seattle WTO protests of 1999 as part of contact improvisation's lineage. In all three of Foster's examples, different expressions of identity are at stake: from Blackness and racial equality to homosexuality and health care justice to global class and socioeconomic struggles. See also Susan Leigh Foster, "Choreographies of Protest," *Theatre Journal* 55, no. 3 (October 2003): 395–412.

9. *Betye Saar: Uneasy Dancer* (Milan, Italy: Fondazione Prada, 2017), back cover.

10. Quoted in email from Julie Roberts to Yinshi Lerman-Tan, October 20, 2023.

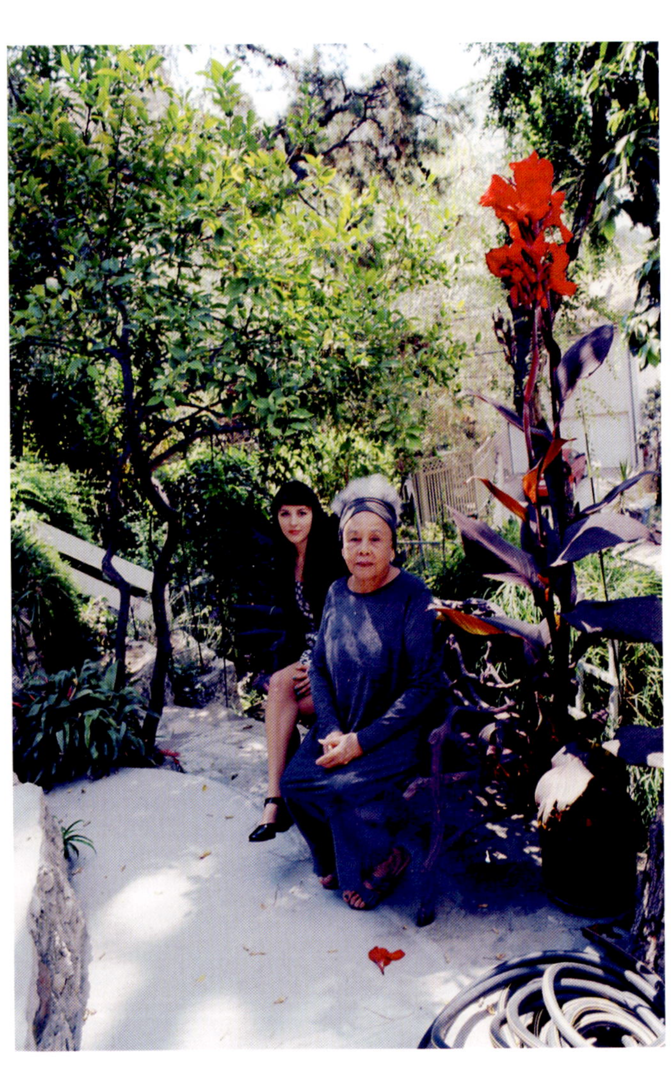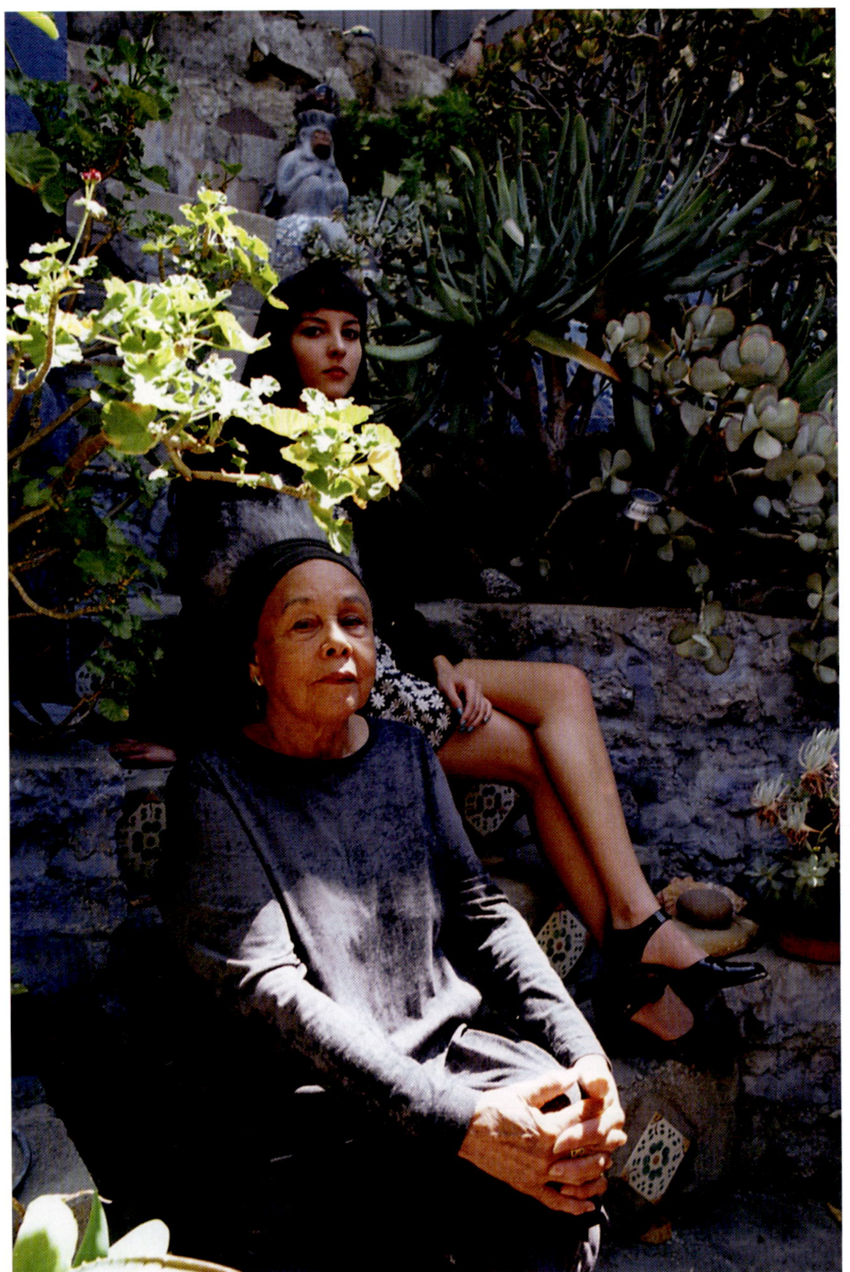

SÓLA SAAR AGUSTSSON

GRANDBETYE'S MEMORY GARDEN

AN ORAL HISTORY OF BETYE SAAR IN PASADENA

One of the fondest memories I have of my grandmother is an afternoon driving through the neighborhood in Pasadena, California, where she grew up. She lived in a house on Pepper Street a few doors down from famed baseball player Jackie Robinson, who was then the local paperboy (p. 85). She showed me where he lived, where she went to school, and where the invisible color line that divided Black and white households once existed. Born in 1926, Betye grew up during the Great Depression and learned to make the most out of what her family could afford. Even as a young child, she liked to collect things, a practice that eventually led her to incorporate found objects into assemblages and art installations. It was this philosophy of collecting and reusing discarded items that she would carry with her throughout her artistic career and personal life.

Her artistic practice parallels the process of gardening, as nature is the original recycler of organic matter. On the grounds of her house and studio, on a quiet, narrow street in Laurel Canyon, she has a marvelous garden. Situated on a hill, it is sprawling, lush, and on a small scale, organized by color. Near her back patio, she created a "blue grotto" from broken dishes and glass a couple of decades ago, a subtle ode to the Watts Towers, which inspired her interest in assemblage art (see p. 68). On her front porch, she's started a "yellow garden." She still enjoys learning about plants and tending to her garden.

Betye's first fine art museum experience was visiting The Huntington in the 1930s, when she was in junior high. It is fitting, therefore, that at the age of ninety-seven, she debuted an artwork that not only was commissioned by the first museum she visited, but also incorporated her interest in gardening by including plant material sourced from the Huntington Botanical Gardens. While Betye has included natural elements in her installations throughout her career, *Drifting Toward Twilight* is unique in that the organic matter was foraged from the landscape directly outside the museum walls, grounding the artwork in the space it inhabits.

Drifting Toward Twilight is a room-size immersive installation that plays with lighting and gradated blue walls to evoke twilight, cocooning the viewer in an environment both earthly and uncanny. With caged

Betye Saar in her garden with granddaughter Sóla Saar Agustsson, 2016

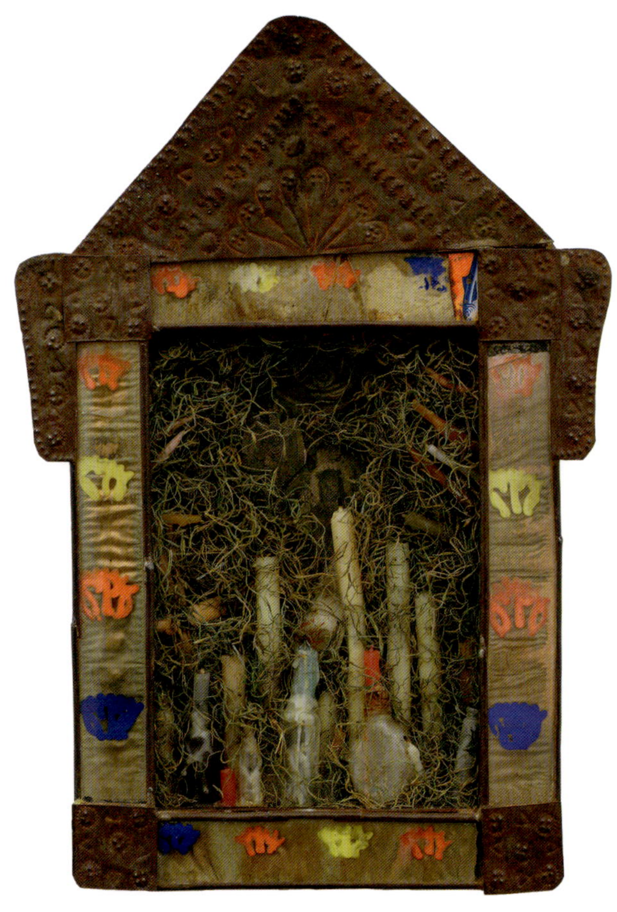

Betye Saar, *Garden Reliquary*, 1989. Mixed media assemblage, 18¼ × 13 × 2 in. (46.4 × 33.0 × 5.1 cm). Courtesy of the artist and Roberts Projects, Los Angeles

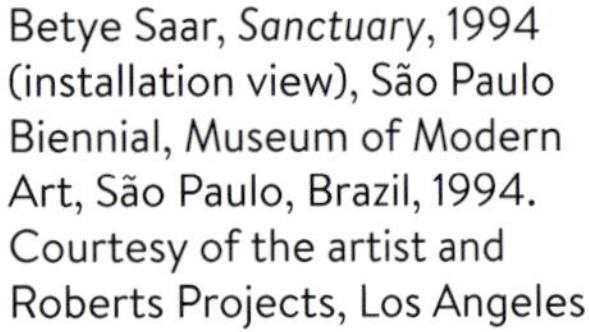

Betye Saar, *Sanctuary*, 1994 (installation view), São Paulo Biennial, Museum of Modern Art, São Paulo, Brazil, 1994. Courtesy of the artist and Roberts Projects, Los Angeles

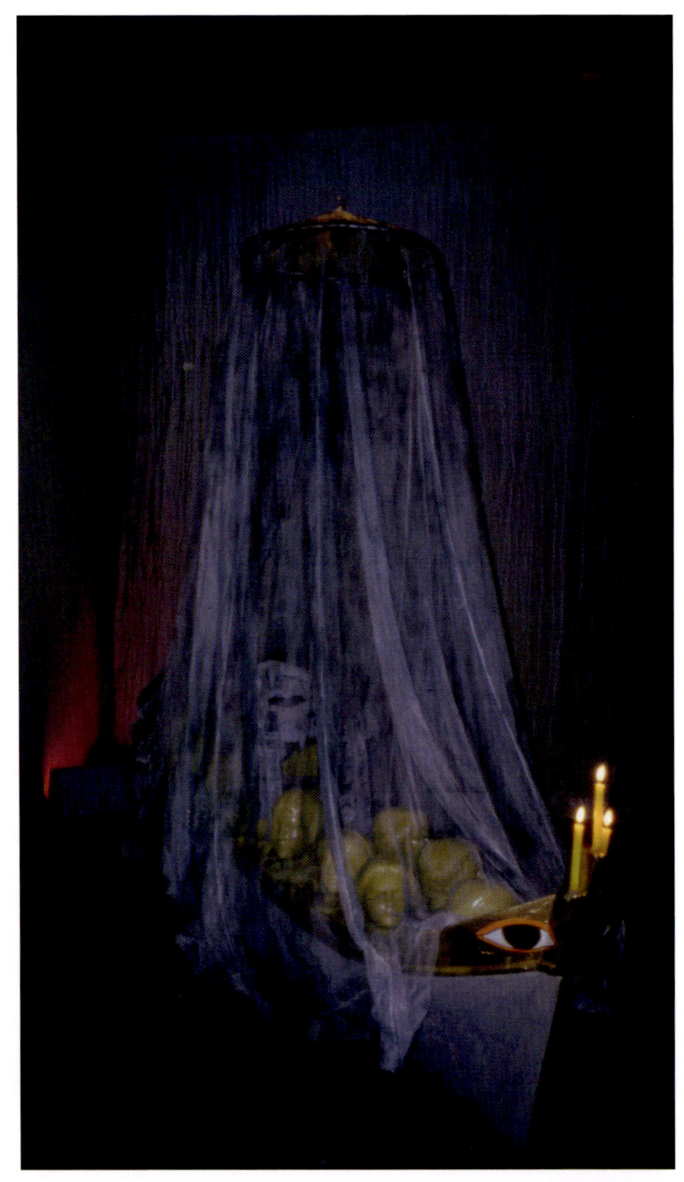

BETYE SAAR

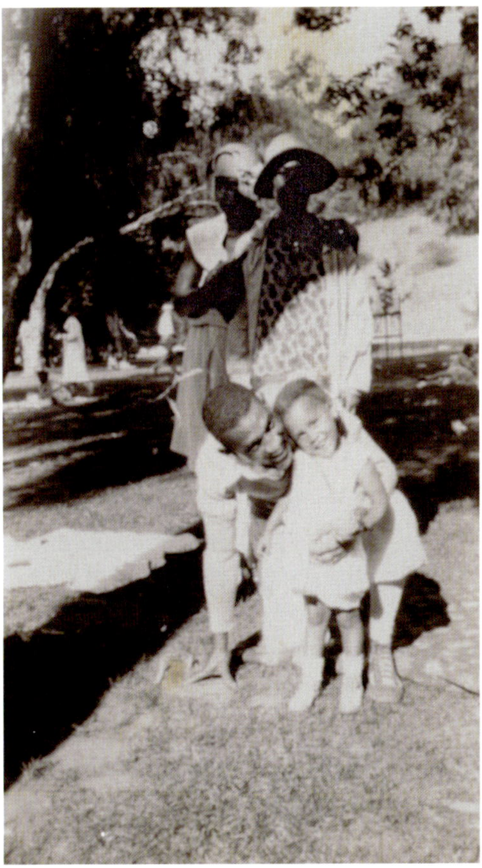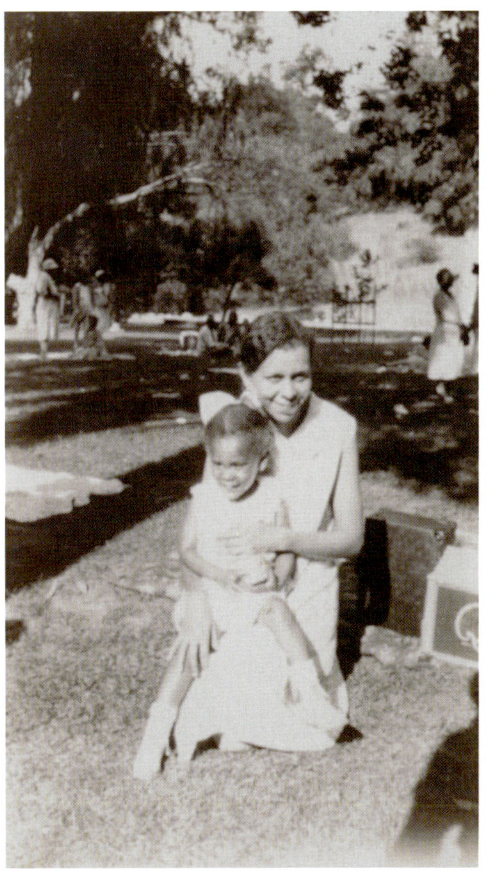

Betye Saar with her father, Jefferson Maze Brown (left) and with her mother, Beatrice Lillian Brown (right), ca. 1929–30. Courtesy of the artist

antlers as passengers in a canoe that floats atop branches, the work suggests an aquatic journey both confining and transformative, recalling her *CAGE* series, which deals with themes of enslavement and civil rights in America (see p. 64). It alludes to the idea that memory and progress are not always linear.

When I worked as Betye's studio manager from 2018 to 2021, she was in the process of collecting antlers and fake plants, scouring flea markets as she began to envision and construct the canoe. I soon thereafter began working at The Huntington, where the canoe would find a perfect home at an institution where the beauty of art, the natural world, and archival materials converge. This installation combines themes of her previous canoe works while also creating a mood and environment that feels distinct from her other works, one that is dreamlike and surreal, built from antlers and plant material and repurposed objects anthropomorphized in a space that moves toward both the past and the future.

As a component of this exhibition and its accompanying documentary film, I conducted an oral history with Betye in her studio in February 2023, during the period when she was making the artwork for The Huntington's commission. She speaks about her early childhood and artistic process. The conversation has been condensed and edited for clarity.

     DRIFTING TOWARD TWILIGHT

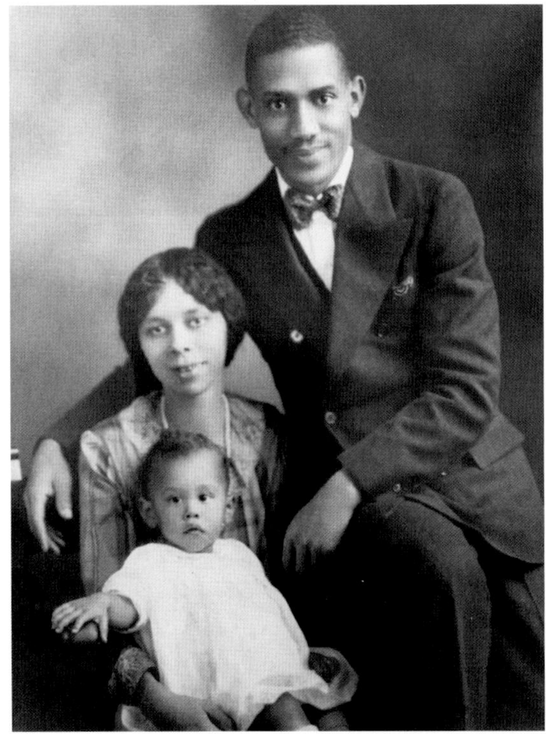

Betye Saar with her parents, Beatrice Lillian and Jefferson Maze Brown, ca. 1926–27. Courtesy of the artist and Roberts Projects, Los Angeles

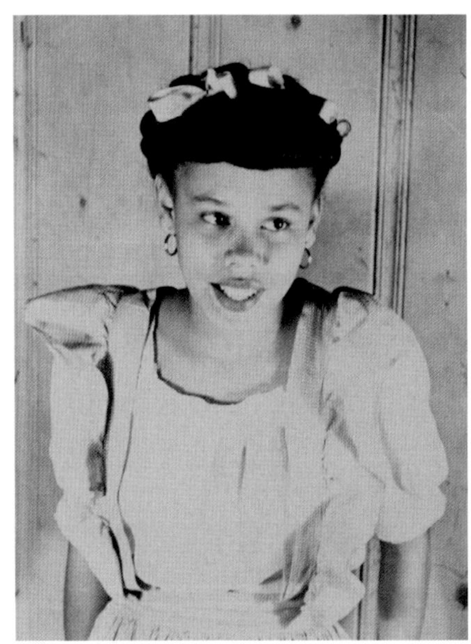

Betye Saar on "Bow and Sucker Day" at Washington Junior High School, Pasadena, California, ca. 1942. Courtesy of the artist

SÓLA SAAR AGUSTSSON: When did you move to Pasadena?

BETYE SAAR: I was born in Los Angeles. My father had a job with an insurance company, and they had a branch in Pasadena. I don't remember exactly how old I was, five or six years old.

SSA: Can you tell me about your early childhood there?

BS: I was the eldest of five kids. I was two when my mother had another baby. We always lived in a house with a yard. I was always curious about things. Whenever we moved to a new house, I would first go to the trash to see what the other people, the previous owners, had thrown away. So, I began collecting at a very early age, maybe like four or five. It wasn't called collecting, it was just "finding stuff," as my mother would say. And eventually that stuff became art.

SSA: Did you know from an early age that you wanted to be an artist?

BS: Now, when you're four or five, you don't know what being an artist means. But I always liked drawing with Crayolas and painting, and those were gifts that my parents gave me. So, I had no idea at that time that I would be an artist.

SSA: Did your parents encourage you to make art, or did they think you should do something more practical?

BETYE SAAR

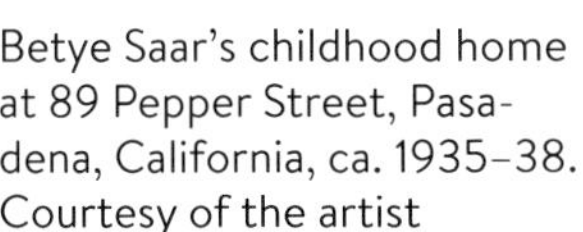

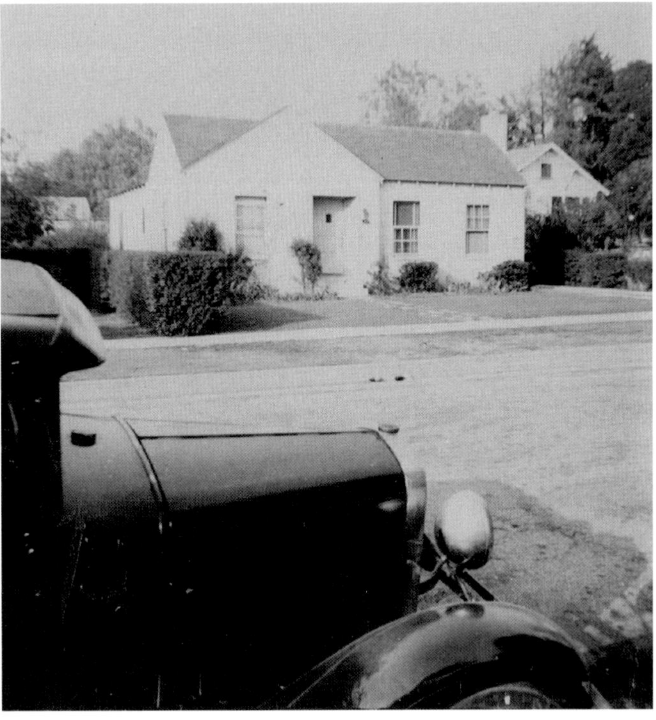

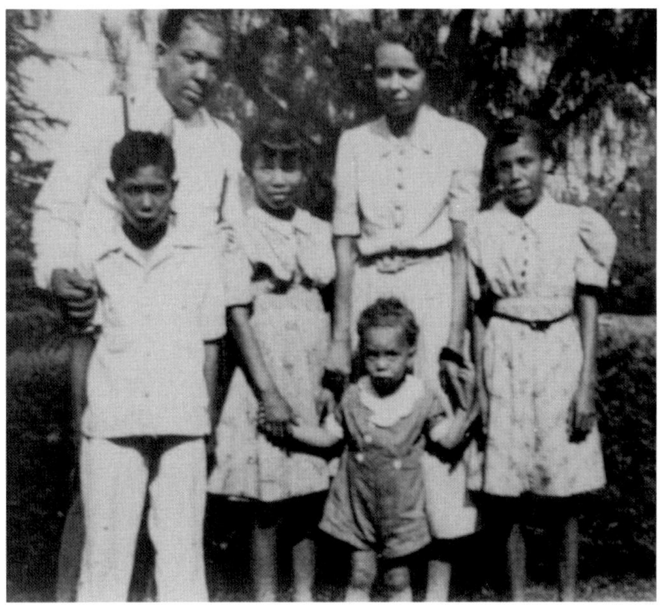

Betye Saar's childhood home at 89 Pepper Street, Pasadena, California, ca. 1935–38. Courtesy of the artist

Betye Saar (far right), with her stepfather, Emmett Trowell; mother, Beatrice; and siblings Robert, Jeffalyn, and Emmett Jr., 1939. Not pictured: sister Sharon Trowell. Courtesy of the artist

BS: Well, I was the eldest of three children at that time, and my mother was busy being a mother. So, anything that would keep me out of her hair was welcome, and drawing was one of those things—drawing and painting. But I also liked to look at things. I liked to look at nature, plants, and gardens. So, I was also filling my head with things that eventually would be subject matter for my art.

SSA: Where in Pasadena did you first live?

BS: The first place that I can remember living in Pasadena was at a house sort of above the Arroyo on Forest Avenue. And it was a small little house where, then, I was the only child, when I was a baby, where I lived with my mother and father. I lived between Pasadena and Los Angeles a lot during my early childhood until my father got a permanent position in an office. And then when he passed away, we moved to where my grandmother, his mother, lived down in Watts. And I

know that in the early 1930s, that's where we were living, in Watts, because I remember there was a very heavy earthquake in Long Beach.

SSA: Do you remember going back when the Watts Towers were being built? How old were you?

BS: It was at another time when we had to live with my grandmother, it was when her husband died, and I moved in with her to keep her company and I went to school. And going to school, I passed the area where the Watts Towers were built. I think they were on 107th Street. I was always very curious about them, about what they were and why they were being built. But, you know, nobody would take me by to look at them. And that didn't happen until later, much later on, when I was maybe like twelve or thirteen, and I would walk to school, and I would walk by and take a look at them. But I was always fascinated by the Watts Towers. In fact, I didn't know anything about art or

DRIFTING TOWARD TWILIGHT

sculpture and that was my first introduction—seeing the Watts Towers.

SSA: When you were living in Pasadena, did your mom ever take you to the Huntington Botanical Gardens?

BS: Yes. I went there. My mother had a friend named Leona who had been our neighbor in the 1920s. And she came to visit us and took us to The Huntington gardens. It was the home of some wealthy people, who had built really beautiful gardens where they collected lots of plants from all over the world. And they took me along. I was maybe like twelve or thirteen at that time. And I remember The Huntington gardens. Dirt paths. There was a paved street, but on the path to the garden was just dirt and plants, which were not really labeled. It was a place where lots of interesting plants were, and it was enjoyable to see those plants. Later on, as an adult when I went back, I could recognize some of the plants that I saw as a teenager at that time. It really stimulated my interest in gardening and in different kinds of plants. When I was a student in school you could elect the kind of science that you took. I was not interested in physical science like physics or chemistry, but I always selected life sciences like botany, and I found a chance to really explore what plants were like and how they grew and how they looked and everything.

SSA: So, when you went to The Huntington, do you remember the art museum? Going to see the paintings there?

BS: Yes, because the first time I went, I think they had just acquired *Blue Boy*, over one hundred years ago. And it was the 1930s, so when it was still a new acquisition. Yes, and it was really important, you know, because it was something from England, because the States weren't really connected to Europe at that time. That was the first time I went to like a formal museum, except for field trips as a kid, but then we went to the Southwest Museum when we were studying Native Americans. So that was something really special, and to walk around The Huntington and see the sculptures in the garden and to see the paintings and the artworks. That was like my first introduction other than a school experience to seeing art separate from a school project.

SSA: And you said you saw a Joseph Cornell show at the Pasadena Art Museum in the late 1960s?

BS: Yes, yes. The Pasadena Art Museum was a small little building that the city sponsored. And I went there, I think the first time I went there, I went with my brother, who was not particularly interested in art, but he was willing to drive me there and I saw the work of Joseph Cornell. And I was just really impressed with how you could take scraps of paper and pieces of odd things and put them together and make a piece of art. He created collage and kind of early assemblage as an artist. And he created these things to entertain his brother, who had cerebral palsy. And it was like a form of entertainment, but then it developed into an art form, and it was different than drawing and painting

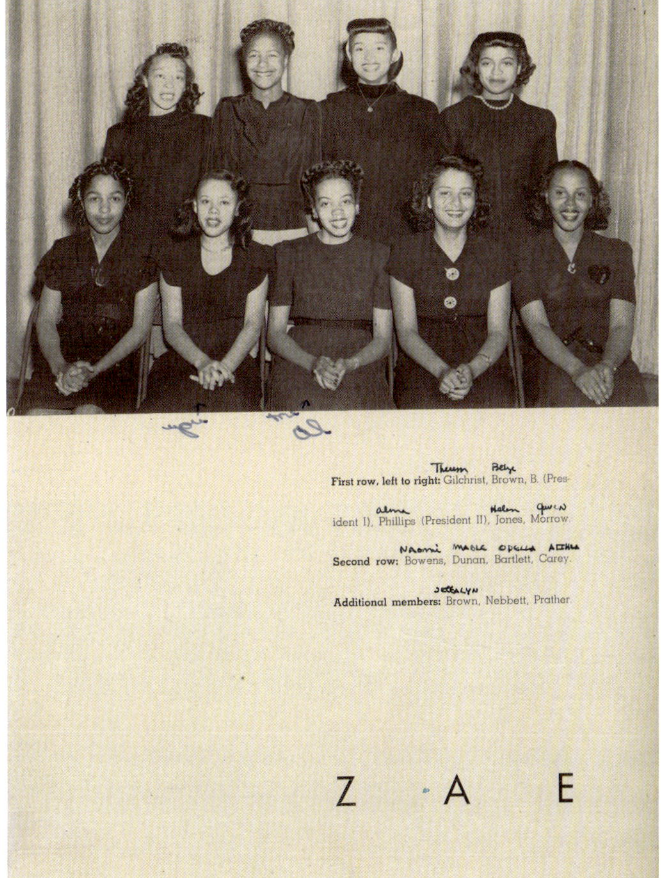

Betye Saar (bottom row, second from left) in the yearbook for Pasadena Junior College, now Pasadena City College, 1946. Courtesy of the artist and Roberts Projects, Los Angeles

and sculpture, but more like a combination of all those activities. And that really impressed me, and I said, I can do that. And for three years I collected things to make collage and assemblages. During that time was the Black Revolution with Dr. Martin Luther King, the murder of Dr. Martin Luther King. And then I had a reason to use this technique. And that kind of got me into the fine art business because it was exhibited in museums and so forth.

SSA: Can you talk about your experience as a junior college student?

BS: I went to Pasadena Junior College the first two years of college. It had two campuses, one near my house and then the other near a house where I had lived before. And I was interested in plants at that time, too. And the science class that I took was always botany, but my focus was art. In the fall, we would always start out by designing a float for the Tournament of Roses because that's what's happening in Pasadena. I never took sculpture. I was really interested in design, like costume design or interior decoration, and when I went to UCLA, as a junior, my major was interior design.

SSA: Did you ever design a Rose Parade float?

BS: Yes, once I got third prize for designing a float because all the students had to design a float. That was part of our curriculum, to design a float. And I once won third prize, which was maybe one hundred dollars or something like that. And that was nice to know that I could make money out of making art.

SSA: Do you remember what the float looked like?

BS: No. It was probably, well, whatever the theme was because every year they had a different theme.

SSA: What kind of art classes did you take first at Pasadena Junior College?

BS: I took design classes, general design, which is considered commercial design now, like designing a book cover or designing illustrations for a book or designing furniture, clothing. At one time I thought I would be a costume designer or clothing designer. So, I studied that.

DRIFTING TOWARD TWILIGHT

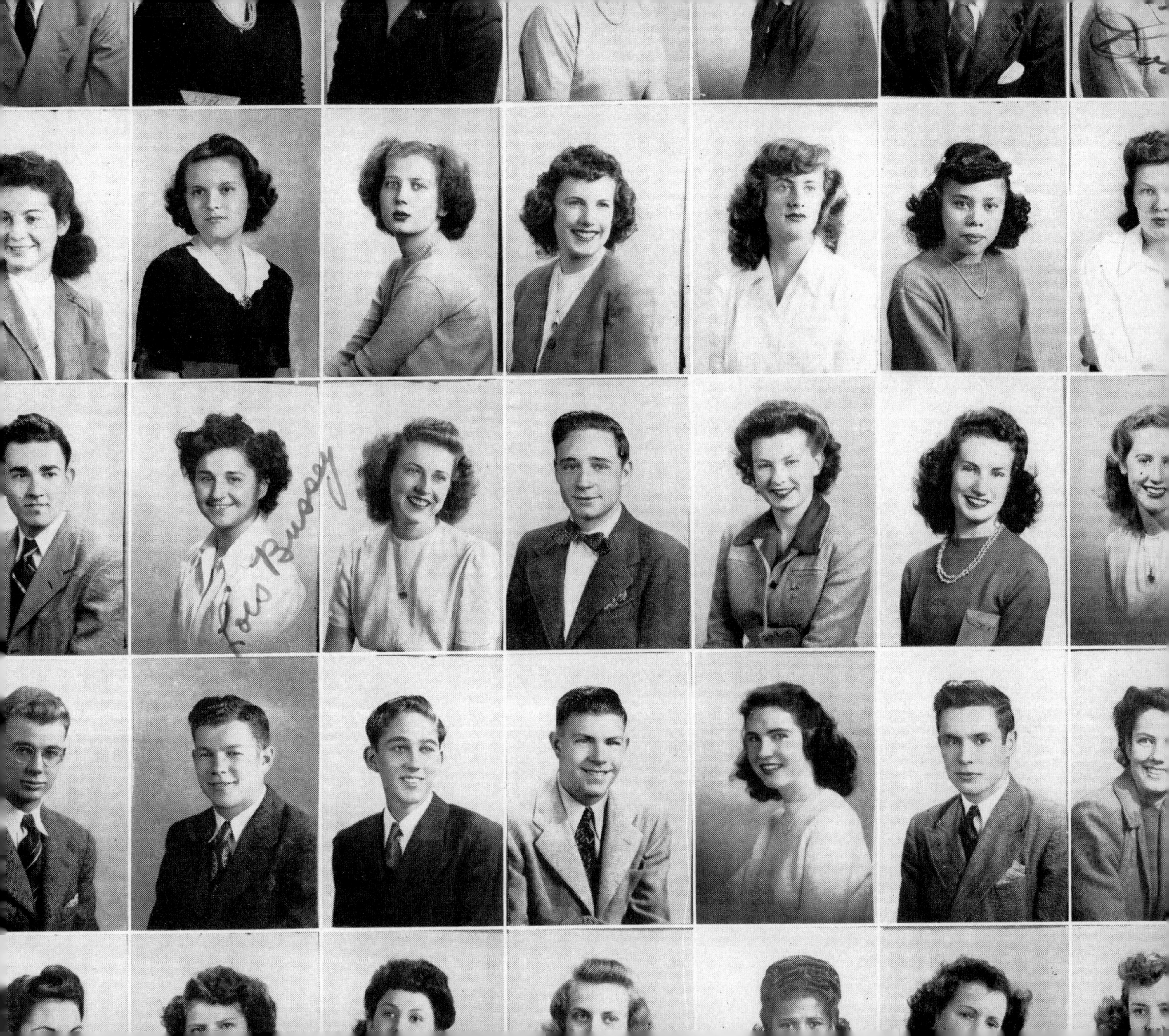

Lois Bussey

SSA: You did do some costume design, right?

BS: I later designed some costumes, but by then I had graduated from school. After two years at Pasadena Junior College, I entered UCLA as a junior and had two years at UCLA. And then, that was also my major, design, but it was designing products and books. I was really interested in book illustration at that time.

SSA: I found this yearbook (p. 87), and I see that you were in a sorority?

BS: Yes.

SSA: Can you talk about that?

BS: Well, they're just like clubs, you know. We got together and we had a little social club before then and then we decided to be a sorority. We were just friends anyway and so we wanted to be in the yearbook. So, we got together, and we all wore black dresses and took our picture, and here we are in the yearbook.

SSA: Were there any hazing rituals or any initiations?

Betye Saar (top row, second from right) in the yearbook for Pasadena Junior College, 1944. Courtesy of the artist and Roberts Projects, Los Angeles

BS: Oh yeah, we did the regular kind of Greek thing of being invited to be part of the club and then we had certain initiations, for like doing silly things like running down to the ocean at midnight and taking a swim and, you know, those torturous kinds of things.

SSA: Torturous?

BS: Yeah, well, that's the way of sororities and fraternities, where, you know, you had to prove yourself sort of crazy to join. But then after a while, you're accepted, and you get to do it to another person. It just goes on and on.

SSA: What did you do after you graduated from UCLA?

BS: After UCLA, I got married and had children and so forth. Before my marriage, I designed cards, greeting cards. That was when the greeting cards that we have now, at that time were called a special name for a card that was just designed by an artist. And I liked doing that because I could still express my art ideas and they would be printed . . . and sent off, even sold, you know. That's where I made petty cash, so to speak. I was married at that time, and designing greeting cards for occasions like having a new baby or getting married or "a fine feathered friend" or something like that. At that time, greeting cards were very popular. It was a way of communicating. And I liked doing that.

And I was part of the commercial art scene, so that meant that I was a commercial artist and made some money at that. And I had an enamelware company with Curtis Tann (p. 90). Curtis Tann, he

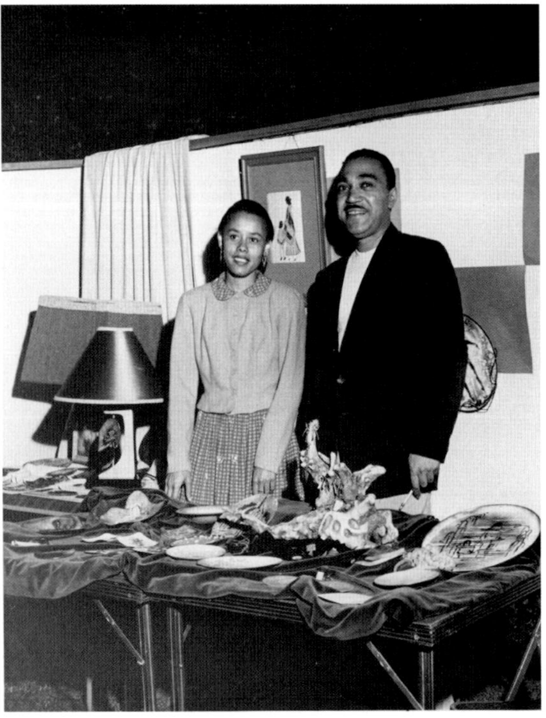

Betye Saar with Curtis Tann, Pasadena city art fair, 1950. Courtesy of the artist and Roberts Projects, Los Angeles

worked for a jewelry design company and started designing jewelry. That seemed to be a way that I could use my art as a way of supporting myself.

I was interested in designing costumes and after I was married and had children, I wanted to work, and I went down to a theater and told them that I wanted to be a costume designer. I had never had any experience in that, but when I was a girl, a young girl, my mother was a seamstress and my sister and I had been taught to sew, so I knew how to sew, and I was an artist. So, I got a job at the Inner-City Theater Company designing costumes. And I really liked that. That was fun to do.

SSA: When did you start doing visual art?

BS: I got tired of doing costumes. And also, because I started to paint and things, and I thought that would be fun to be a painter. And then I had met some people who were jewelers and I worked with them.

SSA: When you married Richard Saar, my grandfather, is that when you moved out of Pasadena?

BS: Yes, I moved out of Pasadena. First, we lived at the beach, Hermosa Beach, and then after that I wanted to be more in the Los Angeles area because there were galleries beginning to develop. Then there were movies to go to and theater, and I love theater design. So, my husband and three kids in the 1960s moved to the house where I live now in Laurel Canyon. I think one of the smartest things that he did was to move to Laurel Canyon because it is very rural and surrounded by nature and I've always loved nature. And yet I had a place to live in a big house, and I made art in my kitchen.

SSA: I've heard stories about when you had a printing press, you had the tub of the liquid for printmaking in your kitchen, and my mom didn't know if it was dish-washing liquid or some chemical.

BS: Well, that's when the technique of tie-dye became influential and easy to do. And I would do things with my children, dyeing fabric, dyeing pieces of paper. So, when my three daughters were young, they were maybe like nine to thirteen or something like that, we always had projects to do. You know, making paper, dyeing paper, drawing. And that was when the county of Los Angeles didn't have many museums here, or galleries. But I would take them to classes there and so forth, and art became a major part of our life.

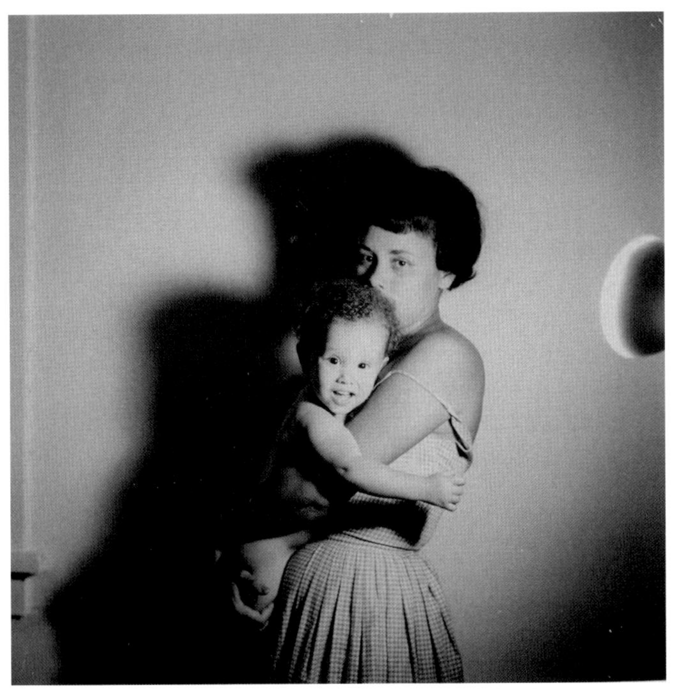

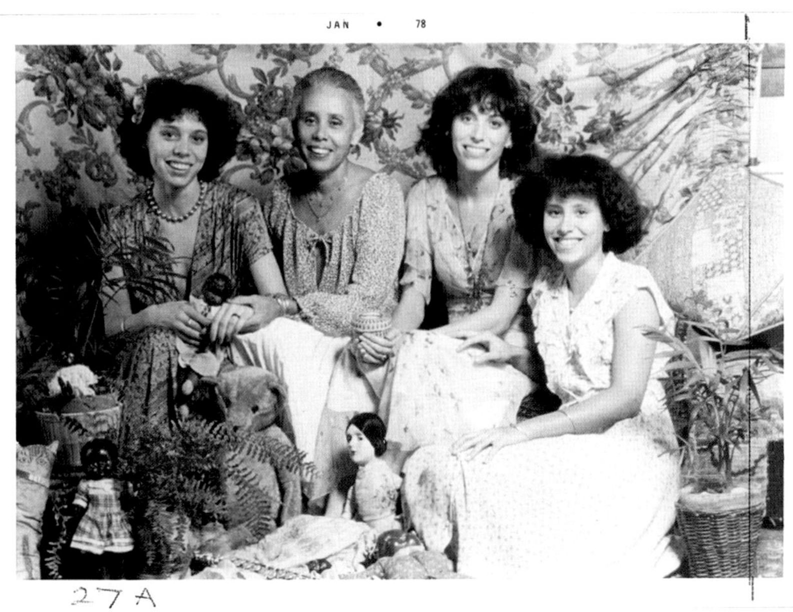

Betye and Tracye Saar, ca. 1962. Courtesy of the artist

Betye Saar with her daughters, Alison, Lezley, and Tracye, Los Angeles, January 1978. Courtesy of the artist and Roberts Projects, Los Angeles

SSA: You said once that being an artist and a mother are close to the same thing because they're both about creation?

BS: Well, because they are both creative and art was a way to keep my daughters interested in different things and to teach my daughters different things. Physically they are quite different, you know, one hurts more than the other.

SSA: Which one?

BS: Well, having children. But art was a way to entertain my children. That was when I first began to be interested in not so much just design, but other kinds of art. But I never felt really qualified to be an artist, to express my thoughts and feelings like that, until the 1960s with the murder of Dr. Martin Luther King. And that became such an issue for me emotionally, and yet I didn't have any way of expressing it except I found out that I could use negative and derogatory symbols that supported racism and turn them around to be a positive thing. Like the first piece I did was called *The Liberation of Aunt Jemima* (see p. 38). Aunt Jemima was a character invented by the white race to show Black women—to show Black people—in derogatory positions of being servants. And it was my feeling that I could make Aunt Jemima into a soldier, into a hero. And so, I did this piece that started me on my whole art career or my lifestyle as an artist. And just taking negative things and turning them around to be positive and to use art as a way of communicating.

SSA: How did you meet Ishmael Reed?

BS: Ishmael Reed was a writer who was doing the same kind of thing of Black America coming into its own creative self, into films and theater and art. I had an art exhibit in the Bay Area, and he attended, and he said, "I write about what you make art about." So, we became friends.

SSA: When did you acquire your first canoe to use in your work?

BS: Well, I moved from making art on paper and very small pieces into art installations where I would have a whole room where I could just express a feeling or an idea of something. At that time, I was also invited to exhibit in other countries, and that meant that I couldn't take a lot of art materials, but I could always go there and go to secondhand stores in another country and find things and create a room-size installation expressing the feeling. I was really fortunate that I got to go to Taiwan, the Philippines, Malaysia, and New Zealand, to all sorts of places. And also here in the United States, I began to do more installations to create a feeling that when you went into the gallery, you became part of it by just looking at the things that I had in there.

My latest focus has been the canoe, which is an object of early America. And I bought this canoe from an ad and shipped it out to my studio in the garage, which is still to be finished. The idea of a canoe, a primitive way of transportation, of moving, is more like the concept of moving from one place to another, from one emotion to another emotion, using one sort of material and changing it to another way, another kind of material.

SSA: Can you talk about the piece you created for The Huntington?

BS: *Drifting Toward Twilight.* It's a poetic title. The inside of the boat is quite beautiful wood, but the outside is just ordinary. I'm going to paint the outside and the walls to match it so that it's installed in a space that suggests water, like it's underwater. So, it would, for the viewer, conjure up all sorts of strange things. First of all, what is she doing with a canoe in a room? But I had a special feeling, more like a dream kind of feeling with the lights and neon. I used something from each environment.

SSA: Do you ever make art from dreams that you have?

BS: Not real dreams because I usually can't remember those. I like organic materials. I like rocks, branches, sticks, things like that. I used water someplace in South America. I had a canoe and I filled it with water or something like that.

SSA: Real water or resin?

BS: Real water.

SSA: And in previous works you incorporated the slave ship diagram (facing page). Is that sort of a theme with canoes?

BS: Yes, yes, I would paint the slave ship diagram on the floor if it were a cement floor. If it were wood, they would leave a stain, but I would have a drawing of it. This slave ship can be enlarged to be under a simple canoe boat, to refer to slaves being brought to America. So, in a way there would be a kind of political issue about my work that would come into an installation. And also, lighting was important. I used neon. I made some neon pieces that had lines or designs. A squiggle

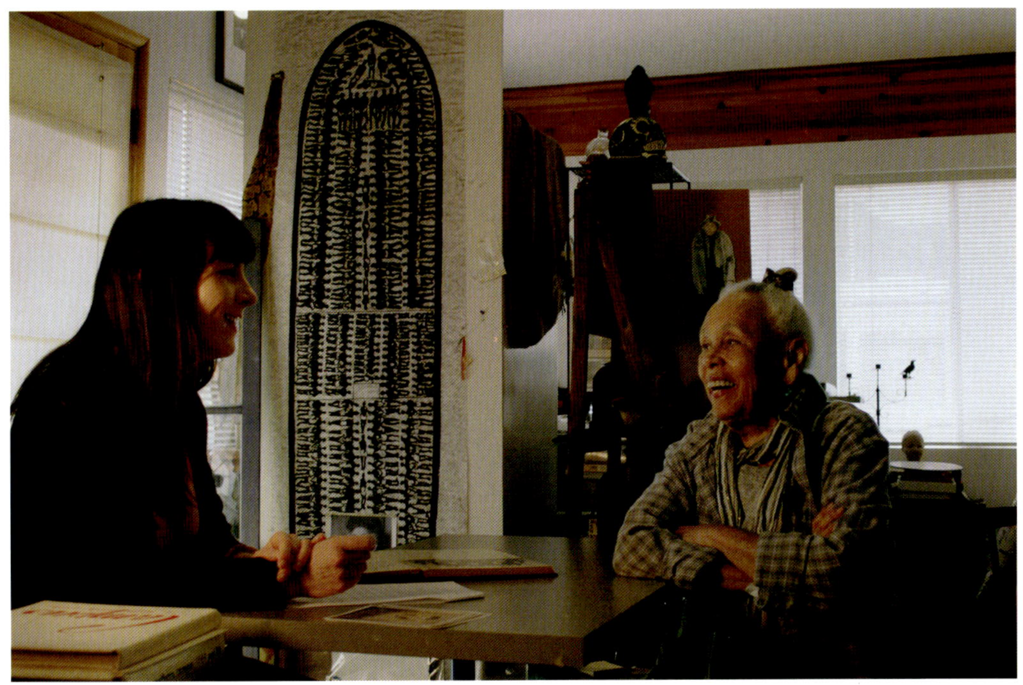

Sóla Saar Agustsson and Betye Saar. Film still from *Betye Saar: Drifting Toward Twilight* (dir. Kyle Provencio Reingold), 2023

of a neon light so it would have this glow to a piece, to the installation (see pp. 52–53). The canoe also just suggests a journey and is kind of a narrative.

SSA: Did you have a story in mind for this canoe?

BS: No. Not that literal. I wanted to use materials that would suggest a narrative to the viewer, or that they could make a part of a story. Like a feeling—it would be mostly the feeling. It is something that's really hard to do in any art form . . . to get an emotion. But certain materials can give you emotions, and somehow using a boat, even if it's over sand, gives you a kind of emotion about being alone or travel or something like that, transportation.

SSA: And you want the light to change and dim?

BS: Yeah, so it kind of pulsates so you can feel that happening. So that it feels like time, like the passage of the day. From afternoon to twilight, and twilight to night or something. You know, not that it goes totally dark, but you know, when you're in twilight, it's always changing. The sun has gone down and the light has disappeared, and it's beautiful. So, it'll give the room the feeling of almost like you're outside, but you're inside.

SSA: Because of the natural materials, there will be a little bit of the garden in the gallery.

BS: I hope to be able to contact some of the gardeners and have them save some of the things that they throw away—dead branches, dead leaves, dead flowers and things in the installation. They get a second chance at life. It isn't every weed that can do that. I want to convey that even in death, those things can be really beautiful. When put together with certain things and with certain lighting, it becomes more of an emotional kind of communication.

My mother loved gardening, so I just grew up learning to love gardening, too. And the people who work here, and say, I'm in this show. This is my weed. I love that, I love incorporating everyone.

SSA: You're helping us build the community across The Huntington. Sometimes we don't always talk to the gardeners, and the art museum is sometimes separate. So, your work is really bringing them together.

BS: I'm glad. Well, it's a special place. It's a really special place. Another reason I'm excited about doing it is because I want, what I would just like is for young people to fall in love with The Huntington and to want to go, not just for a school assignment or something like that.

SSA: Can you talk about the materials you used in the canoe?

BS: The inside is quite beautiful, the natural wood, so I'll leave it like that. But eventually I may paint the outside a color wash or something like that. But right now, it's just sitting here, gathering things, and getting my ideas together of what I would like to show. These strange things—I think they're finials, these odd shapes here, that I have added horns to, chairs with cages with horns (see pp. 50, 51).

Other than just the fact that I like the way they look, it is also a way of incorporating plant life. I like combining manufactured objects with natural objects. And antlers are one of the favorite things that I've used. And actually, even this strange object is a natural object that grows on a tree [a cypress knee]. When I have been a visiting artist in many schools, especially schools in the East, I have asked if they have a rowboat or a canoe or something because I like to use it in my installations. Underneath, I usually have fabrics or branches, and that way I can always incorporate something from the vicinity of where I'm working. Like I know in one place in Australia, it was near the seashore, so I had my students gather driftwood or rocks or something like that to use underneath the canoe. Usually it's like dead branches, driftwood, growth. When I do the exhibition on the campus, I want to use maybe discarded plants or branches or leaves or

foliage from the campus itself to put underneath the wood, sometimes underneath the boat. Piles of rocks, but I like to incorporate something from the location to be underneath the canoe. And in the gallery, sometimes I have sand, if it's a cement floor.

SSA: Can you talk a little bit about the birdcages?

BS: Yes, they're made in Taiwan, new but meant to look vintage (see p. 47). I like the shape. In my studio, I do have cages. I like the idea of having something that's free because of the space in between it, but still a cage. And I guess it would reflect back to my ideas about slavery, of being taken care of and having certain things, but you're still caged. You're caged into slavery. Like caged freedom, in a way.

And then I just like physically the way they're shaped, the way they look. I love them in this work.

SSA: Last time I was here, you talked a little bit about water and the canoe capturing the process of water gliding and drifting.

BS: Because water is a natural thing that I like to use and there were very few installations where I've had a chance to do it. I believe once when I was in Australia, I was near a stream and . . . we used rocks to build something in that stream.

Sometimes it's the ocean and we collect things from the ocean, but I like to include the natural elements of water, earth, air, fire. I can't use fire, but I can use a photo of fire or a painting of fire. In other exhibitions, I had the canoe suspended from the ceiling so it's like about three or four feet off the ground, so it looks like it's either floating or moving. In this installation I will have it on a bracket or something because it can't be suspended from the ceiling, but still not touching the ground.

And this is *Drifting Toward Twilight*.

SSA: What's it like making art at the age of ninety-six?

BS: Am I ninety-six?

SSA: You don't look it.

BS: I don't know. I keep thinking, Well, what am I going to make when I'm a hundred? You know, I try not to think of the number. The number is not important.

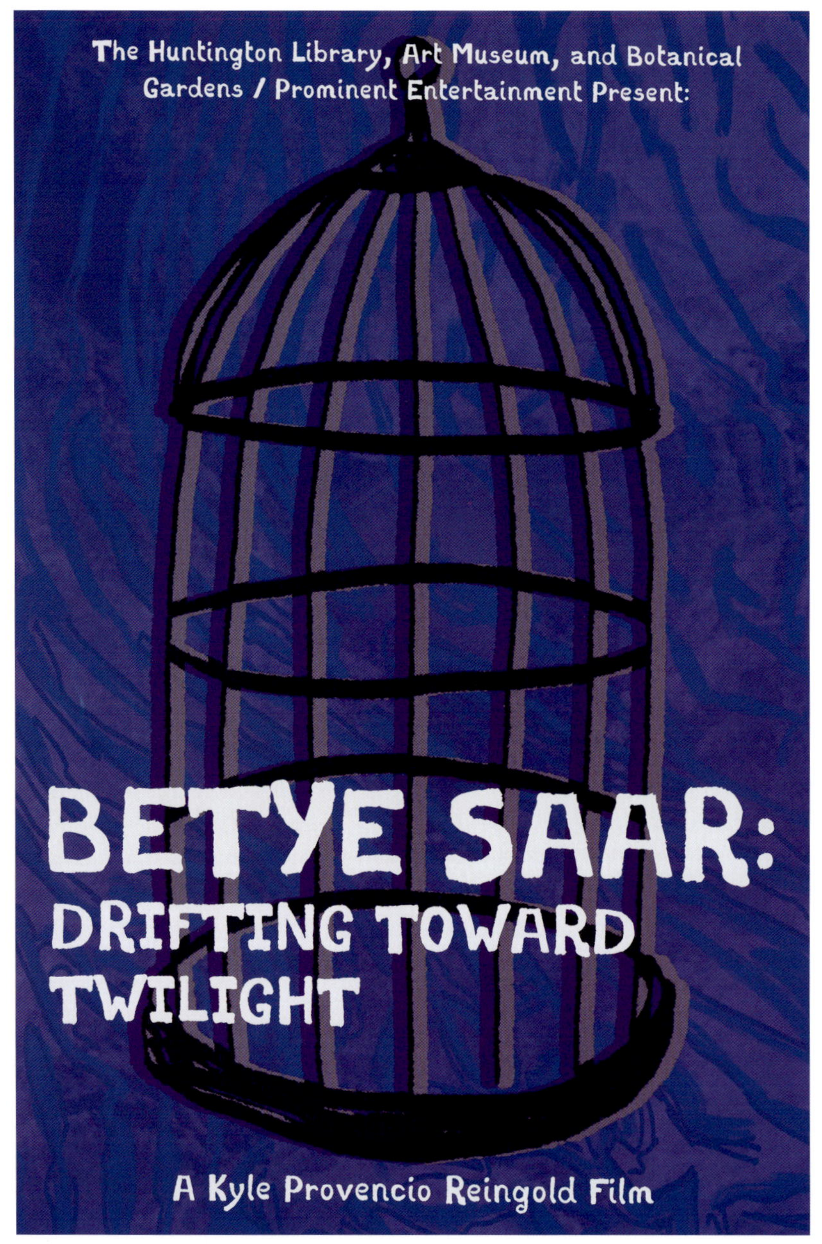

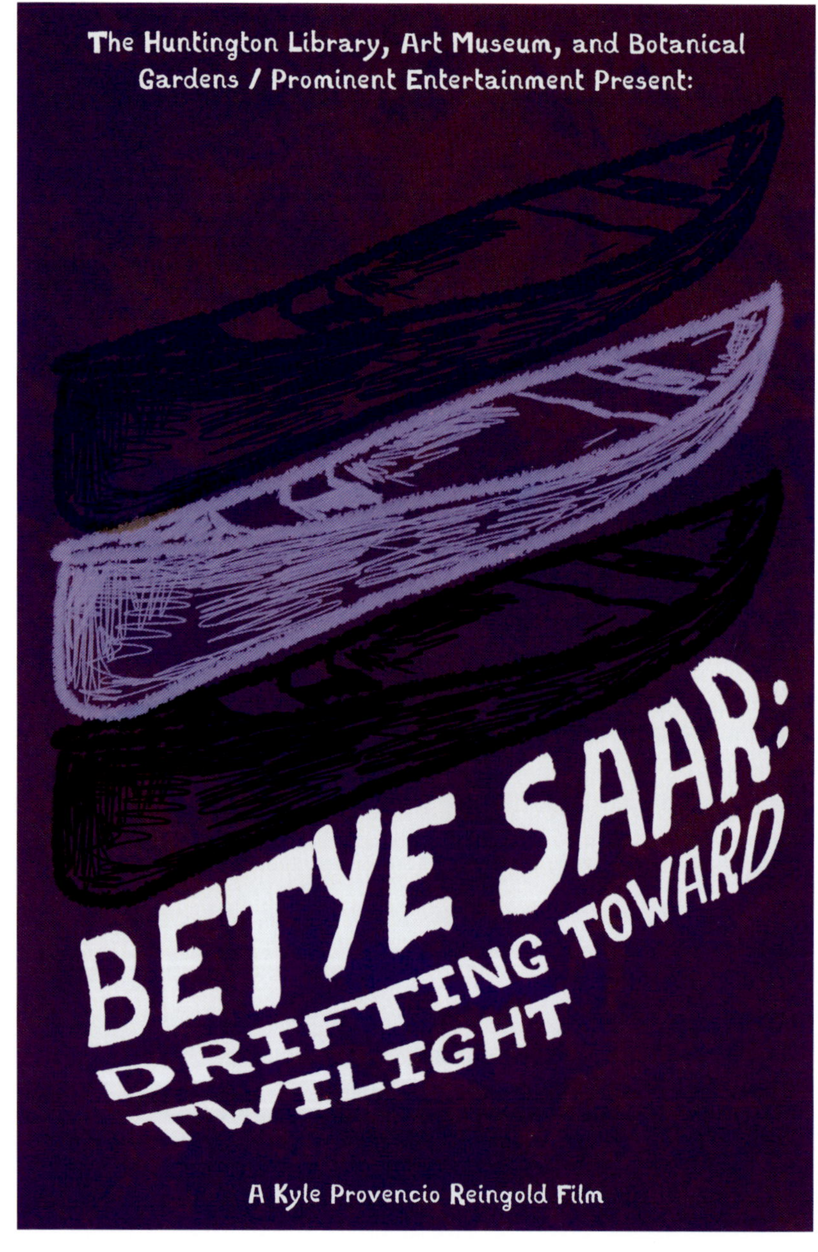

Laila Núñez for YAYA Studio, posters for the film *Betye Saar: Drifting Toward Twilight*, 2023. Digital image

BETYE SAAR: DRIFTING TOWARD TWILIGHT (2023) FILM STILLS

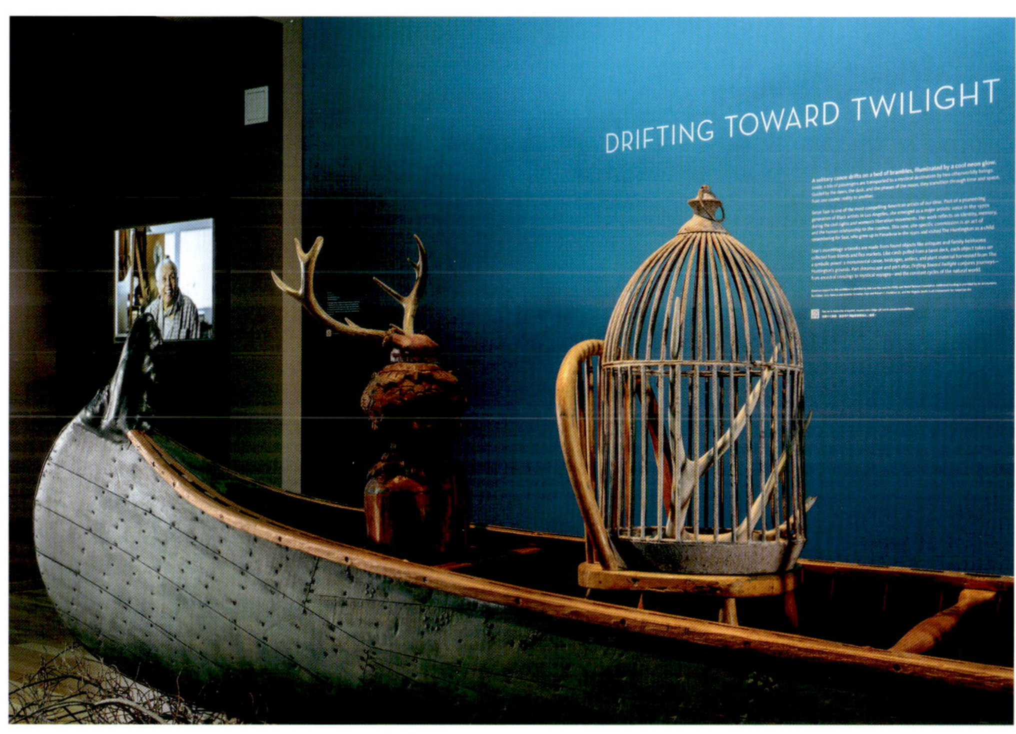

The Huntington commissioned a short documentary film, directed by Kyle Provencio Reingold, to accompany Betye Saar's installation at The Huntington. The film includes parts of the oral history conducted by Sóla Saar Agustsson, in which the artist discusses her early childhood, her career, and the work in progress in her studio. The film also captures her process of harvesting natural materials from the grounds with Robert Hori, associate director of cultural programs at The Huntington.

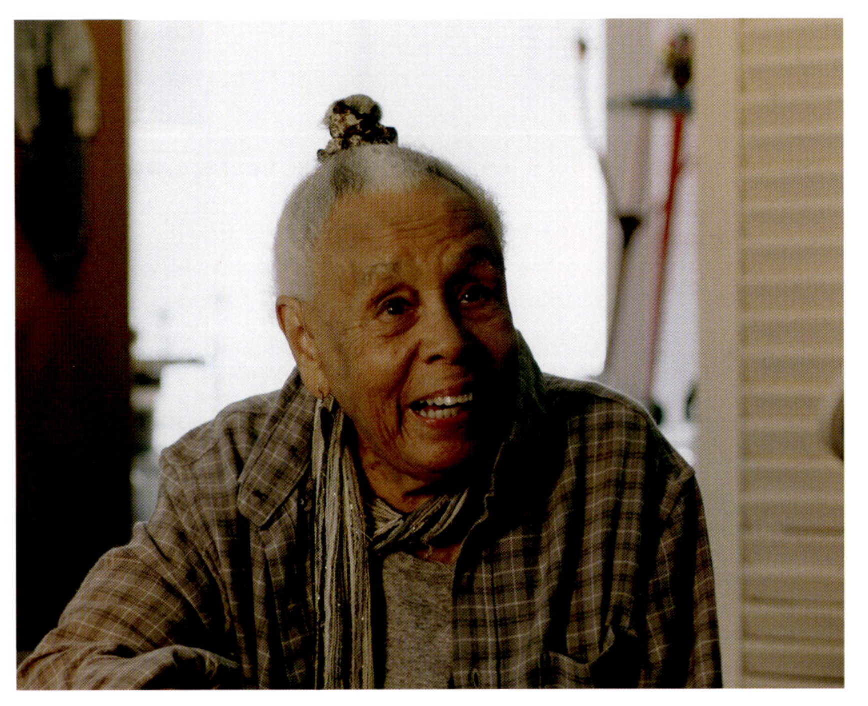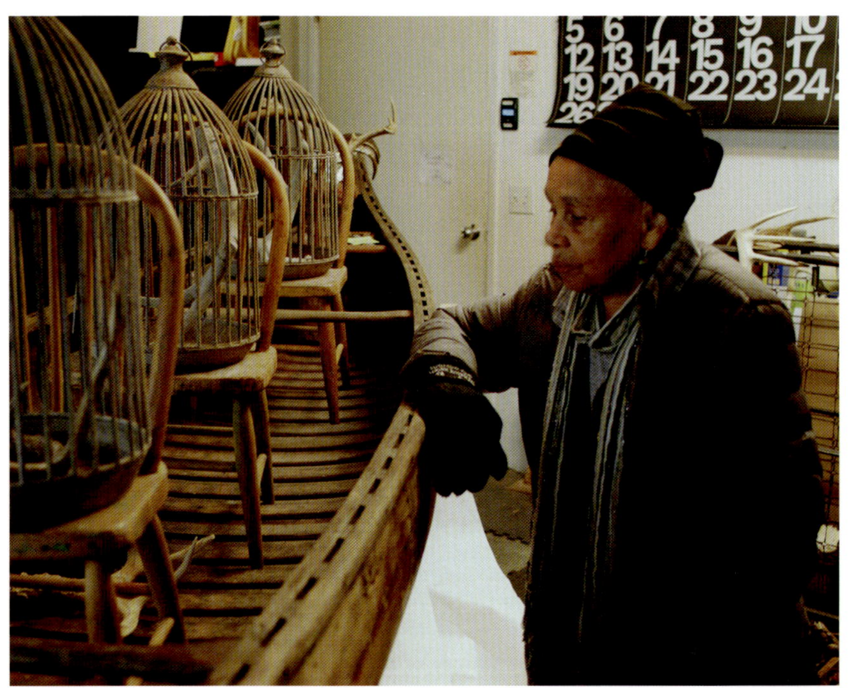

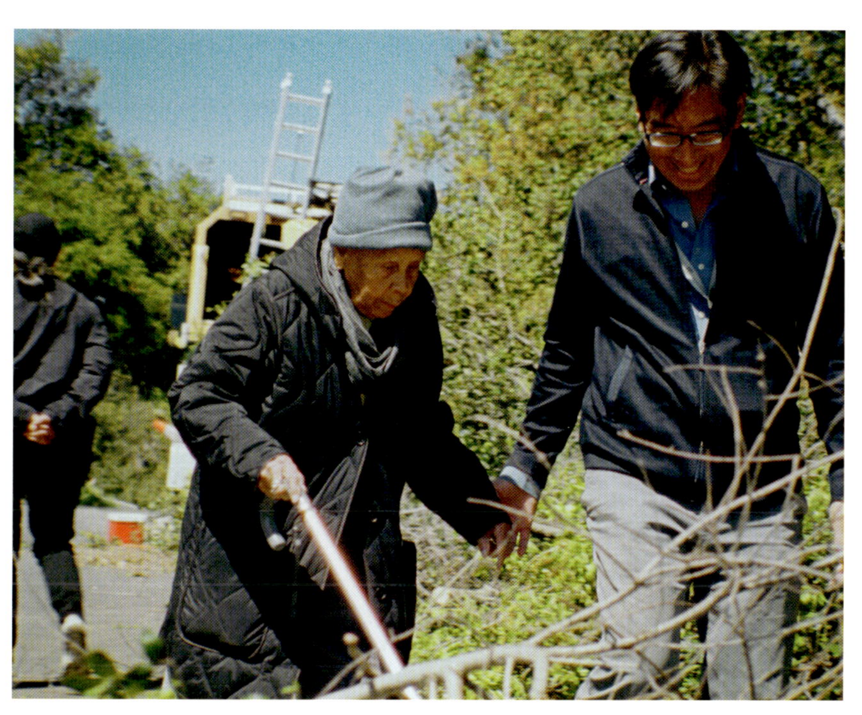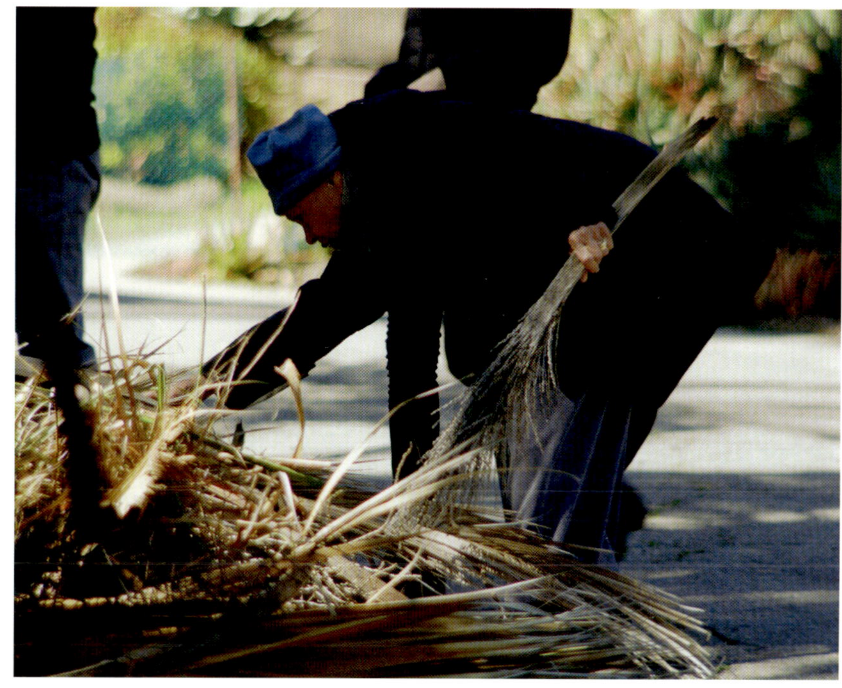

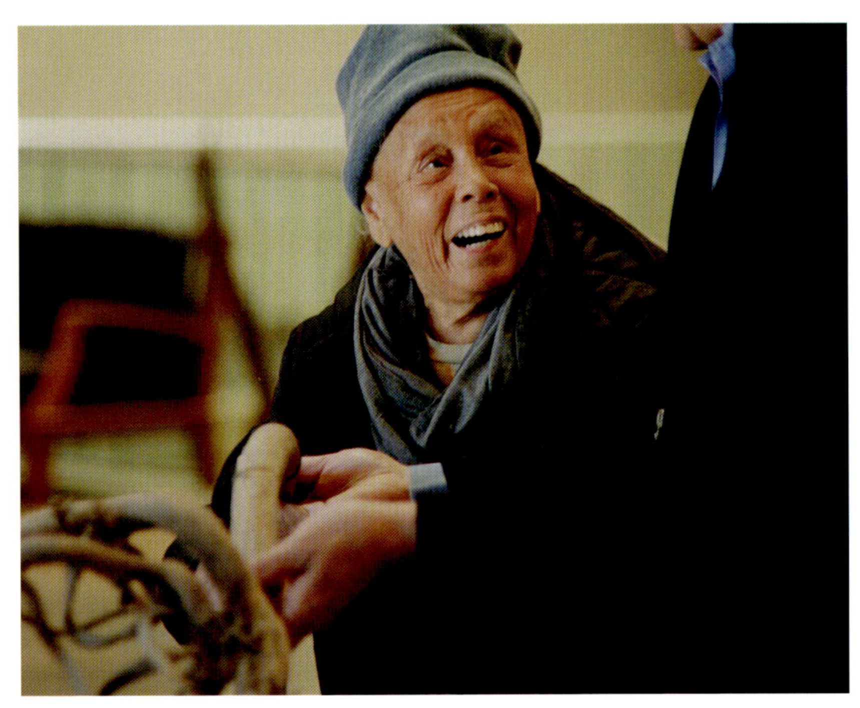 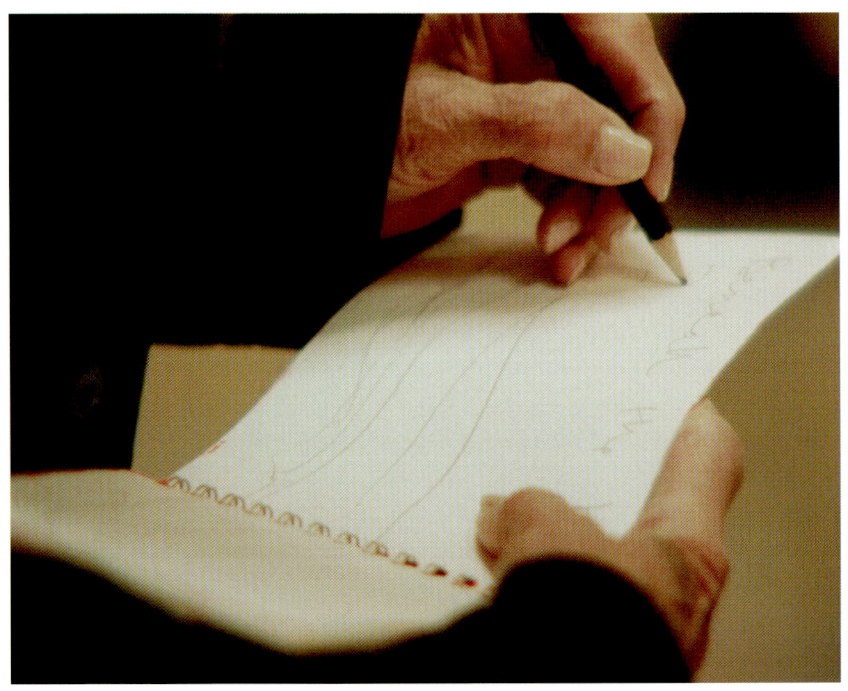

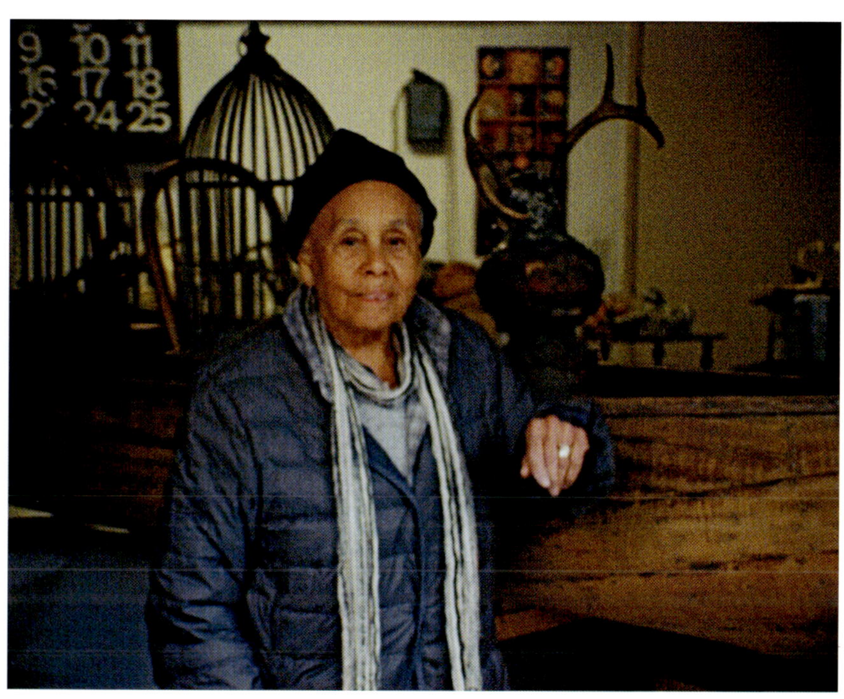

Betye Saar: Drifting Toward Twilight (2023). Digital video, 16mm film, still photographs, archival video, animation, sound; 16 minutes, 30 seconds. https://www.youtube .com/watch?v=c0n2Dg3C10Y.

Directed by Kyle Provencio Reingold.

Featuring Betye Saar and The Huntington gardeners.

Presented by The Huntington Library, Art Museum, and Botanical Gardens / Prominent Entertainment.

A Pocho Pictures Production. Produced by Gloria S. Álvarez and Kyle Provencio Reingold.

Cinematography by Daniel Cho, Jessica Muñoz, and Kyle Provencio Reingold.

Edited by Neil Howard Butler.

Interviewers: Sóla Saar Agustsson, Yinshi Lerman-Tan, Robert Hori, and Kyle Provencio Reingold. Co-producers: Sóla Saar Agustsson and Yinshi Lerman-Tan. Animation: YAYA Studio. Colorist: Ale Amato. Production sound mixer: Miguel Ángel Rodríguez. Post-production sound mixer: Jason McDaniel, Electric Audio, Inc. Color by Primary. Producer: Alex Zhao. Head of production: Diane Valera. Executive producer, color: Christina Roldan. Color assists: David Oh and Matthew Stepanek. Post-production supervision: Hubcap House.

Original motion picture score composed by Joel M. Ross. Performed by Joel M. Ross's Good Vibes Quintet: Joel M. Ross on vibes and keys, Gabrielle Garo on flute, Josh Johnson on tenor saxophone, Jermaine Paul on bass, and Jonathan Pinson on drums. Score recorded at East/West Studios, Los Angeles, CA © 2023. Studio recording engineer: Tyler Shield. Score mixed by James Tuttle. Joel M. Ross appears courtesy of Blue Note Records.

ILLUSTRATION CREDITS

All Betye Saar images and artworks © Betye Saar, courtesy of the artist and Roberts Projects, Los Angeles

Art Institute of Chicago / Art Resource, NY: page 42

Benjamin Blackwell: page 38

David Butow: page 14

Sophie Caby: page 80

Harlan Feltus: page 91 (right)

Brian Forrest: page 64 (left)

© Isabella Stewart Gardner Museum / Bridgeman Images: page 60 (left)

© 2024 The Joseph and Robert Cornell Memorial Foundation / Licensed by VAGA at Artists Rights Society (ARS), NY: page 42

Pierre LeHors: page 74

© 2024 Museum of Fine Arts, Boston: page 65 (top)

Digital image © 2018 The Museum of Modern Art / Licensed by SCALA / Art Resource, NY: page 26

Bob Pace: page 90

© Ishmael Reed, reproduced by permission: page 17

Tennessee Reed: page 19

Kyle Provencio Reingold: pages 93, 98–101

Lezley Saar: page 36

Richard W. Saar: pages 39, 68, 91 (left)

Tracye Saar-Cavanaugh: page 10

Saar studio: page 59 (left)

Paul Salveson: pages 17, 73, 76, 77, 79, 82 (left)

David Sprague: page 58

Unknown photographer: pages 6, 16, 18, 22 (right), 23 (left), 24, 25 (right), 26, 29 (top), 40, 59 (right), 63, 70, 72, 82 (right), 83, 84, 85, 87, 88

Robert Wedemeyer: pages 22 (left), 25 (left), 32, 60 (right), 62, 65 (bottom), 66 (top), 78

Joshua White / JWPictures.com: pages 2–3, 13, 46–55, 97

David Wong: pages 23 (right), 29 (bottom)

YAYA Studio: page 96

CONTRIBUTORS

SÓLA SAAR AGUSTSSON is a fiction and arts writer, an artist, co-curator of *Drifting Toward Twilight*, and Betye Saar's granddaughter and former studio manager. Her work has been featured in publications such as *East of Borneo*, *Flaunt*, and *Hyperallergic*.

HILTON ALS is a staff writer and theater critic for the *New Yorker* and associate professor of writing at Columbia University. Als was awarded the Windham Campbell Prize in 2016, and he won the Pulitzer Prize for criticism in 2017.

TIFFANY E. BARBER is a scholar, curator, and critic whose work spans abstraction, dance, fashion, feminism, film, and the ethics of representation, focusing on artists of the Black diaspora working in the United States and the broader Atlantic world. She is assistant professor of African American art at UCLA.

YINSHI LERMAN-TAN is the Bradford and Christine Mishler Associate Curator of American Art at the Huntington Art Museum and co-curator of *Drifting Toward Twilight*. She is a scholar and curator of American art and visual culture, and she received her PhD in art history from Stanford University and her BA in American studies from Yale University.

CHRISTINA NIELSEN is the Hannah and Russel Kully Director of the Huntington Art Museum.

ISHMAEL REED is an American poet, novelist, essayist, songwriter, composer, playwright, editor, and publisher. His latest play, *The Shine Challenge, 2024*, premiered at the Theater for the New City, New York, in 2024.

First published in 2025 by the Huntington Library, Art Museum, and Botanical Gardens

Published in conjunction with the exhibition *Betye Saar: Drifting Toward Twilight*, organized by the Huntington Library, Art Museum, and Botanical Gardens, on view November 11, 2023, through 2027.

Available through:
ARTBOOK | D.A.P.
75 Broad Street, Suite 630
New York, NY 10004
www.artbook.com

For The Huntington:
Project management by Jean Patterson
Publication coordination by Shirin Sadjadpour
Principal photography by Joshua White

Produced by
Marquand Books, Seattle
www.marquandbooks.com

Copyedited by Tanya Heinrich
Proofread by Ivy Long
Designed by Thomas Eykemans
Typeset in Brandon by Tina Henderson, Miko McGinty Inc.
Image management by I/O Color
Printed and bound in Singapore by Pristone

This commission and its presentation were made possible by Mei-Lee Ney and the Philip and Muriel Berman Foundation. Additional funding was provided by an anonymous foundation, Terry Perucca and Annette Serrurier, Faye and Robert C. Davidson Jr., and the Virginia Steele Scott Endowment for American Art.